Maria Martinez with her pottery. Photo: © Jerry Jacka Photography

Creating with Reverence

Art, Diversity, Culture and Soul

Claire Campbell Park

SOTOL BOOKS

This book is dedicated to Mom and Dad, Tad and Thea,

whose love and support are with me always.

Library of Congress Control Number: 2009910775
ISBN: 1-4392-6204-7

SOTOL BOOKS
Tucson, Arizona

Front Cover:
Reverence VII
coiled waxed linen and cotton, with rock
2 1/4" x 17 1/2"x 17"
artist: Claire Campbell Park
photo: J. Keith Schreiber

Contents

Introduction

The lives and work of the artists who have inspired this book present a global, inspirational and timeless perspective of art. They represent diverse cultures, yet share common values. Their art is a commitment to community, heritage, and faith. Their position is one of integrity and of service to humanity, and reflects a mature and unselfconscious sense of reverence, humility, dignity, and gratitude. These artists impress me with the depth of their focus, as they consciously integrate all aspects of their lives with the substance of their work. They challenge our values and cultural perspectives, affirm the importance of the creative process, and increase our awareness of the relationship between art and life. This leads to an inspired and fulfilling creative foundation applicable to any endeavor. Their perspective is in keeping with the needs of our shrinking world and is not limited by the predominantly Western European, psychoanalytic, and linear perception of contemporary art, so often championed by critics and art historians, which tends to glorify the individual and the "new."

Contrary to what it claims, too often contemporary art appears to be the exaggerated, egotistical statement of the iconoclast, over rating the importance of the individual, rather than an act of enlightenment or service. It is only in the very recent history of Western European culture that art has become more commonly viewed as something outside of community, outside of daily life; often bombastic, nihilistic, and narcissistic - isolating art and artists - rather than reflective, connecting and nurturing. I find that the lives of the artists in this book inspire approaches to art and life that are a powerful antidote to this modern malaise. I have shared their stories with fellow artists (including those who create for museums, galleries, home and community), students, teachers of art, art patrons and creative people of many other disciplines. I found that they also receive great inspiration and support for their creative commitments and that the dialogue that ensues is challenging and rejuvenating.

Creating with Reverence is structured so that at the beginning of each chapter you will be introduced to the life and work of artists such as Maria Martinez, a Pueblo potter; the Mayan weavers of Chiapas, Mexico; and Aboriginal artists recently introduced to acrylic paint. We also consider woodworkers in Kyoto, Japan, who create implements for the tea ceremony; the grandson of a Croatian immigrant who created a carousel in Missoula, Montana, to honor his grandfather's struggle and his adopted country; and women in Indian villages who make ground paintings for their families and communities.

The artists' stories are followed by questions that allow you to consider your own perspectives and insights, and further develop your own creative foundation. Questions such as: How is art integrated with your life? What is most important to you, the process of creating or the product, and why? What ideas and values are represented in craftsmanship? What do your clothes signify? How can your art work be an expression of community? What does an act of total attention mean to you? Do you focus on what is important to you when you create?

After presenting the questions, I give you my students' insights and my own reflections, from an artist's perspective - personal and experiential - tempered by my own life experience. We consider topics such as the relation of art to a continuity of generations, freedom of choice, objects of integrity, cross-cultural inspiration, concepts of time, the creative process and faith, strength and beauty. In order for you to understand my perspective somewhat better, I will tell you a little about myself and my students.

I have been a working artist for over thirty years. My medium is mostly fiber (textiles), but also mixed. I exhibit nationally and internationally in galleries and museums. Probably the two exhibits I was included in that have most influenced the way I see art are the *International Textile Competition '87* in Kyoto, Japan, and *Made in California: Art, Image and Identity 1900-2000* at the Los Angeles County Museum of Art. *The International Textile Competition* exhibition in Kyoto was accompanied by a symposium that broke the conventional European art boundaries and included those creating "fine art," those working in the Japanese textile and kimono industry, and the highest practitioners of craft - the National Living Treasures of Japan. I was in Kyoto for ten days and the experience supported and deepened my longing for seeing and understanding art in a different light. I did not rest until I found a way to make a second trip to Kyoto in 1995. I feel I have learned much from Japan. *Made in California* also broke boundaries in abundance, between "fine art" and "craft," "mainstream" and "fringe," daily life and "high culture," Western European based art and "other," creating a vibrant cultural dialogue. My own work was included in the 1970s and '80s section, and it was incredible to feel like a small part of this dialogue. The exhibition covered the years in which my great-grandparents, grandparents, parents and brothers and sisters resided in California and helped me to realize how much of the California experience had become a part of who I am, from what my family passed on to me and from growing up and being educated there.

I was blessed to grow up in Southern California during a period that was increasingly aware of and open to diversity. And for as long as I can remember, I have had an interest in understanding the way people from other cultures and backgrounds see and experience life. I received a BA from Scripps College in Claremont in 1973 and an MFA from UCLA in 1978; both fostered a global perspective.

I have had the opportunity to experience many cultures firsthand. I have lectured at museums and universities in the United States and abroad, including the Louvre and Ecole Nationale Supérieure des Arts Décoratifs in Paris, Seian College of Art and the World Textile Conference in Kyoto, Apeejay College of Fine Arts in Jalandhar, India, the University of South Australia, and the University of Tasmania. The connections with people that follow such opportunities - conversations, invitations to artists' studios and, yes, parties - are wonderful. I researched Moroccan textiles in London, Paris, and Morocco, which led to being a consultant for the first major exhibition of Moroccan textiles in the United States, at the Textile Museum, in Washington, D.C. Since my research was mostly hands-on, it also led to many fascinating people and unexpected experiences; such as a pool-shark who became a major Moroccan textile collector and my being an honorary man for an evening at a bachelor party thrown for the son of the head textile merchant of Marrakech. Like many artists, I love to learn through experience; through seeing, feeling, breathing in people and places. I am thankful to have shared a bit of life with people from many countries, cultures, and situations.

Teaching studio art at Pima Community College in Tucson, since 1978, allows me to do just that. I have had the privilege to teach students from eighteen to eighty five; Latino, African-American, Asian, Native American (many different nations), Caucasian; students from Yemen, Iran, Israel, Germany, Spain, Japan, Taiwan, Thailand, Pakistan, South Africa, Mexico, Brazil; students from all over the world. I have worked with students from varied economic situations: some were direct from the homeless shelter, others from mansions in the foothills. Some students had never had any art before and were convinced they were not creative; others were professional artists who had exhibited for many years. I have had students recovering from alcoholism, coma, stroke, and the tragic death of family members. Students with all sorts of learning challenges including dyslexia, seeing everything upside-down, and diagnosed schizophrenia have been in my art classes. I have worked with students who were deaf, in wheelchairs, and legally blind. I have had students suffering from severe arthritis, cancer, and AIDS. Some students come to art to help rebuild their lives after losing a job they had for twenty years or to recover from divorce. My students have been chefs, nurses, doctors, Vietnam and Desert Storm vets, prisoners on parole, hair stylists, teachers, farriers, retirees, home-managers, cowboys, photographers, secretaries, dentists, lawyers, librarians, homicide detectives. People from every situation come to art because it can revive, renew, inform and sustain them. So often in our culture we are challenged to defend the value of art, yet the thousands of students I have shared with in my classes have taught me art's value; each in their own way, with their own unique life. When I first started to teach I resented how much time and energy I spent on "social work," helping students to forge their lives, rather than on art and aesthetics. I was wrong. My students have taught me that the greatest gift of art is the gift of life.

Some years after starting this project, I was having lunch with a colleague who teaches journalism. She had been a hard-hitting reporter for many years and is used to posing challenging questions. She said to me, "My daughter, who wants to study painting, just came back from a trip to Bali. She said artists there are revered by their communities. Why isn't it true here?" I thought it was a good question.

Perhaps artists are revered in Bali because they create with reverence; making art that is deeply connected to heritage, community and faith. My own understanding of what this means comes from all of life and experience. However, faith is my foundation and the lens through which I see all else. I grew up Congregationalist, survived a very brief and ill-considered exploration of New Age spirituality and became an intensely Vatican II Catholic in 1994. I have a great appreciation for what believers of other faiths have to teach me and I am often humbled by their lives, their insights and, as with many of their portraits in this book, their very beings.

Through the stories of artists from many cultures, the questions for reflection, the insights of my students, and my own singular experience, it is my hope that this book will help you to draw anew on your own life experience and paint, weave, write, compose, form, and live your own conception of what it might mean to create with reverence.

All the way to heaven is heaven.
— *Saint Catherine of Siena*

Lady Flowery Face of Our Father - Magdalenas huipil.
Photo: FOXXARCHIVE.COM

Art and Life

The exceptionally beautiful book *Living Maya* demonstrates how the weaving of the Mayan women of Chiapas, Mexico, is thoroughly integrated with their lives. They learn to weave brocaded huipiles (tunics) at an early age and continue to weave into old age. This is a reflection of their heritage, their community, and their faith.

It takes many years to learn how to weave the complex brocade traditional to this region. If a girl is fortunate she will learn from her mother. If not, she may go to study with a relative. The designs have been handed down, generation to generation, for centuries. Highland huipiles have their roots in pre-Colombian culture and some of the designs resemble those worn twelve hundred years ago.

The designs on a huipil are symbolic: they speak of the community's life, history, mythology, beliefs, and connection to the land. "A huipil describes the earth just as the first rains fall, a world in flower" (Morris 1987, 134). The bottom border alone of the huipil opposite depicts the Earthlord creating rain clouds and his assistant the toad, who sings of the coming of the rain. As a girl or a woman weaves, "she is continuing in the path set down by her ancestors, confirming the validity of their teachings with her work" (Morris 1987, 69).

Most weaving is done for the immediate family and each community has its own distinctive style. The most elaborate weavings are ceremonial costumes worn by married women, but young girls often weave the brightest, most eye-catching designs. Inspired weaving is valued by the community. Women within a community can identify each weaver by her style. Most weavers prefer to remain anonymous outside of their community and "sign" their weavings with a design. The signature design of the weaver at the left is "Lady Flowery Face of Our Father" (Morris 1987, 135). Communities stage weaving contests and bring in judges from other villages and towns to encourage quality and stimulate interest.

The process of weaving is highly integrated with faith. Before beginning her first weaving, a girl will light candles and pray to a saint. The saints' statues are clothed in huipiles. In many communities, young women offer their first weaving to their patron saint as an act of devotion. Slus Tonhol, a weaver from Tenejapa, says that in order to master the art of brocade a woman needs divine inspiration from the saints:

I learned to weave long ago. I was a young girl when I
learned. "I'll never learn," I thought to myself. "I'll probably
die first here at this loom before I learn brocading!"
I was really sad that I didn't know how to weave. I began to
pray. I prayed to Santa Lucia (Patroness of Weavers), to San
Pedro, and to San Diego.
Slowly I began to learn. I went two or three times to leave
candles at the church and pray. Then I began to learn little
by little.
Now I know brocading very well. No one ever showed me
how.
I learned with my heart (Morris 1987, 68).

*What do your clothes signify? Do you learn with your heart? How is art
integrated with your life?*

In modern Western culture our clothes tend to signify relatively
superficial aspects of our lives. Clothes can indicate our economic
situation, lifestyle, the function we are going to, our moods, personalities,
sexuality, color preferences, and age. We have many different clothes for
different situations. In many parts of the world, people have traditionally
owned very few sets of clothes, yet what they wear connects them to their
heritage and the shared beliefs and values that are the foundation of their
community.

The Maya can identify a person's community by differences in the
designs used in their huipiles. Most of us are a bit dubious as to who our
community is. The world is becoming our community; a sea of potential,
but one we can drown in. Our ability to identify where a person comes
from by her clothing is becoming rarer and rarer, as the world adopts a
homogeneous uniform.

When a Mayan woman puts on a huipil she is wearing what she
believes. She identifies with her community and reinforces shared values.
When I ask students about what their clothes signify their response is
almost always about being an individual, yet when we look around the
room we realize we are for the most part dressing a whole lot alike. In my
art classes, our clothing seems to be dominantly about comfort and
convenience, with some theme and variation. Comfort and convenience
are the values we appear to be most willing to manifest as a group, yet the
huipil also represents heritage, mythology, religious convictions; values
that demand a commitment to more than the individual.

Wearing something that identifies you with community and reflects shared values gives the wearer a greater sense of responsibility and allows the wearer to live those values more fully. When I started wearing a crucifix to school, students of many faiths shared with me in a new and meaningful way; sometimes challenging, sometimes supportive, but never boring. Once when I needed it (more than usual), several students volunteered to pray for me and a Dine (Navajo) student gave me a blessing from the Great Spirit. This would never have happened in a secular school, without my silent symbol eloquently speaking for me.

Sometimes I fear that what we are coming to believe in is Juicy Couture, Gucci, Nike and other icons of consumerism. This was beautifully reflected by the characters on the sitcom "Clueless" with their dictum "You are where you shop." Isn't it more meaningful to wear something made with love and devotion by someone you know, than to be a billboard for a corporation? How much better to have a few things made beautifully, with care and integrity, respecting limited resources, made to last for decades, through a process that is spiritually meaningful, than to own a closet full of clothes made in factories (or sweatshops) that are intended not to last. Great value can be found in the process and the product when we make something with thought and care by hand for someone we know. Unlike the Mayan people, we rarely wear our heart on our sleeve. We hide what is most important to us or do not know or commit to our foundation. Some clothes give the heart life, strengthen commitment to values that matter, use the earth's resources wisely, and help us to be more complete as we live our daily lives.

What does it mean to learn with your heart? "You can't learn with your heart. It's an organ!" one student declared. But others say you learn with your heart when you are so passionate about something that it carries you along. Some say learning with your heart is learning with a sense of compassion, with a commitment to serve others, a mission. Still others, believe as I do. You learn with your heart when you open it to God, and this is all encompassing.

The Maya of Chaipas, Mexico, are my teachers. Their art is integrated with every aspect of their lives. Art and life are one. They and the other creators in these chapters have profoundly changed my awareness of how art is integral to my own life.

How is art integrated in your life? It is a question as complex as each of our ever evolving lives, but I believe you will find, as I have, that the inquiry is a rewarding one.

Maria and her sister Clara polishing. Photo: Laura Gilpin

Community

Maria Martinez, of the San Ildefonso pueblo, revived Pueblo pottery through exceptional artistic ability, hard work and dedication. In 1907 Pueblo pottery was in a state of decay. In that year, Dr. Edgar L. Hewett began excavations of prehistoric Pueblo sites, and one of the Native American diggers was Maria's husband. Maria became very interested in some of the pot shards that were excavated and began to develop pottery inspired by them. Her first pots were purchased by Dr. Hewett and more orders followed. Maria's work gradually became internationally acclaimed. She received many honors and awards and visited the White House during the administrations of Hoover, Roosevelt, Eisenhower and Johnson. Her success revived the Pueblo pottery tradition in San Ildefonso and neighboring pueblos, and led the Pueblo economy from poverty to relative affluence.

Maria's work is exquisite, but I am equally impressed with her. In the book *Maria*, her son Popovi Da and the author Richard L. Spivey eloquently address the foundation of Maria's contribution.

> Our values are indwelling and dependent on time and space unmeasured. This in itself is beauty. Our first great value is our trusteeship of nature, and this is beauty also. Then there is an order and direction of our lives, a unity, the ability to share the joy of sharing, creativeness and minimum competition. This too is beauty (Da: Spivey 1979, xxi).

> From her point of view, she is a Pueblo Indian woman; nothing more, nothing less...The Pueblo Indian views life as an integrated whole; and all of the parts, working together in harmony, have their place within this whole: family, community, religion, culture, living and dying. Until recently, individual achievement has been a foreign idea to this culture. An individual did not excel; the group excelled. Maria belongs to and is a part of her culture, religion, pueblo, and family. They come first; they have to come first. But there is no conflict. Pueblo Indian ceremonial life is everyday life...When family or friends are in need of help or food or money, she gives, she shares. When she has little, she gives of what she has, saving only the smallest portion for herself. When Maria attained skills as a potter that gave her a

considerable edge over the other potters, she shared those skills (Spivey 1979, 1).

Who comprises your community? Do you serve your community through your artwork?

Maria's life as an artist was community life. How different her example is from the image of the contemporary artist we so often envision. The artist as iconoclast, a glorified individual, who is somehow elevated above and separate from community. When I ask students what their artwork is about, the most common answer I get is self-expression. The individual is of the greatest importance. Very few have any sense of service or the connectedness with heritage and shared values evident in Maria's life and work. However, this begins to change after discussion of the above two questions.

For most of us, our sense of community is no longer all encompassing and immediate as it was for Maria. Our sense of community has become very complex, sometimes overwhelming, to the point that many of my younger students are not aware that they are part of any community at all. An example of our contemporary sense of community is my own. I am a member of many communities that often overlap. I have my immediate family, my husband and daughter; my extended family, large and scattered over the United States and Canada, making it difficult to keep the strong ties we all want; the neighborhood; my work community, students and colleagues at the college where I teach; my church community; my professional art friends, who are all over the world. I am increasingly aware of my part in the global community (as we all are) and the interconnected consequences of every choice I make. A scenario such as this is true for most everyone these days. An anthropologist friend says there is a current theory that our lives are so full of choices and diverse opportunities that we become a culture of one. Although many acknowledge the importance of community, the complexity of maintaining multi-layered and distant community is cause for some to give up; leaving them floundering and in isolation. I have found that by reflecting on this question some students begin to be more aware of community and make choices that will strengthen some part of their complex community. This helps them to feel more connected and a part of something larger than themselves. Maintaining any community takes time and effort. Art is often a lonely and extremely time-consuming pursuit. Yet through awareness of community, many artists have put the two together in rewarding ways.

Do you serve your community through your artwork? For many there will be separate answers for different segments of their community. Some may focus on using their artistic abilities to strengthen their families. Traditional ways include quilts, family memory albums, holiday decorations and costumes, and everyday home environment. One student made a series of puppets for her children. Others may reinforce personal friendships. An example of this is a student who wove a personalized purse for each of her closest friends. As she wove she placed a photo of the friend or a shared memory near the loom. Each purse had textures, colors, images inspired by a friendship. The quality of her focus as she was weaving showed in the finished product. Each purse was exquisite and had its own personality. She reinforced all the positive qualities of each friendship as she wove and had a lasting symbol to give.

Other students have volunteered to help community. A Native American student worked with at-risk youths on a reservation painting murals. Another student drew exciting and imaginative backgrounds for a church carnival. A student in her seventies organized other seniors in an ambitious Noah's Ark mural for her church that took over a year. Another wished to help inner-city children and began a non-profit after-school program that provided art projects with a multicultural perspective and used recycled materials. Two students volunteered to help teach Tohono O'odham fourth and fifth graders to weave and to relate their creations to storytelling. One student returned to a local program for at-risk youth, from which he had graduated, to work as a student aide in a drawing class, mentoring young adults in a situation he understood well.

My friend and former colleague, the internationally recognized photographer Louis Carlos Bernal, created a deeply moving body of work when he turned to his community values for inspiration and captured the soul of Chicanismo in the 1970's and 80's, during a time of great struggle for cultural identity. He had this to say about Chicanismo: "Mexican American is a term used to describe a person who is of American birth, but whose cultural soul derives from Mexico. This dual reality has been a burden which has clouded our identity. Chicanismo allows us to accept our history, but also gives us a new reality to deal with the present and future...to be a Chicano means to be involved in controlling your life. Chicanismo represents a new sense of pride, a new attitude, a new awareness" (Simmons-Myers 2002, 13). For an exhibition catalog published in 1978 he wrote, "I have felt a great deal of anger and anxiety in my life, and I have used photography as an outlet for these frustrations. My images have always dealt with the inner battle of my soul...My images speak of the religious and family ties that I have experienced as a Chicano. I have concerned myself with the mysticism of the Southwest and the strength of the spiritual and cultural values of the barrio. These images are made for the people I have photographed" (Simmons-Myers 2002, 15).

Lou once reflected, "I would say my work is reverent. I find something the way I think it ought to be and preserve it" (Simmons-Myers 2002, 9). A photograph he took in 1988, titled "Angelina," shows a young woman sitting on her knees, on a simple bed pressed against a corner of a room. The surrounding walls are bare, except for a portrait of a saint on one and a montage of family snapshots on the other. She is wearing pink shorts, a slightly lacy top, a crucifix and an unassuming expression that says, "Well, this is me." Yet the photograph belies an undercurrent of warmth and love, the ties represented in the objects she has chosen to surround herself with, and the respect of the photographer. Lou said of the encounter, "Being photographed won't change her life, but she probably feels more beautiful now because someone thought she was" (Simmons-Myers 2002, 8). By making the choice to create with reverence, Lou Bernal gave to the barrio community and helped us all to see, to connect, to overcome the hurt and confusion of prejudice and misunderstanding, and replace it with empathy and a greater understanding of beauty. His life and work reveal grace.

The examples of Maria, my students, and Lou, have inspired me as an exhibiting artist, to more consciously embody community values in my work and to more actively share my creative abilities with family and community, immediate and extended. I am more mindful of what I bring into the world and more diligently question whether it serves my community, local and global. Through this commitment, I experience an increased sense of connectedness and a deep-seated joy.

Maria's life and work were well integrated. Her work came from a strong foundation of heritage and belief. She approached her work with a spirit of respect, gratitude and reverence. She participated in community and gave to the community. She prayed when she worked. Her work was prayer: reinforcing her values through the process of creating and sharing those values with those who viewed it. Her life was prayer.

Chuck Kaparich, Carousel Impresario. Photo: Tom Bauer

Collaboration and Continuity

The making of Missoula, Montana's carousel, as told in *A Carousel for Missoula*, is an inspiring story of collaboration and an awareness of continuity. The story begins with a nineteen year old Croatian immigrant, John Kaparich, who in the early 1900s left his new bride behind and worked for seven years as a smelterman in Anaconda, Montana, before there was money for her to join him in America. Once reunited, they did whatever they could to make a living for their family. The Kaparichs made wine and sauerkraut in the basement to sell. Other people from their community paid to sleep in the family's beds during the day. After many years they had a family portrait taken with their seven children. The boys had on borrowed jackets. The little girl wore her best dress. They sent one copy home because they were proud of what they had achieved in their adopted country, and one copy was kept in the family and passed on from father, to son, to grandson. One afternoon the grandson, Chuck Kaparich, came across the photograph and cried, realizing he had never thanked his grandfather for what he had accomplished.

Sometime later, during a visit to Spokane, Washington, Chuck Kaparich encountered an antique carousel, created by a Danish immigrant named Charles I.D. Loof. This was a turning point for Kaparich. He says, "For some people, it might be walking into a cathedral, you just get that sense of awe. But for me, it was walking in and seeing the kids spinning around on those horses." His grandfather's picture was still on his mind. "All these people like my grandfather and Charles Loof came here to be Americans. They were here to make this country something. It meant something to be an American" (Devlin, Bauer and Engen 1995, 6).

Kaparich did not know where it would lead him but he became "swept away" by a passion for carousels. He read everything about carousels he could lay his hands on and made at least $500 in long distance calls to carousel experts. Eventually it came to him, "If they could do this one hundred years ago, why couldn't someone do it today?...I made up my mind that by God I was going to build a carousel if it took me the rest of my life" (Devlin, Bauer, and Engen 1995, 7). Through his belief in his dream, his determination, and the coming together of a community, it took only five years.

Chuck Kaparich had worked as a gravedigger, a school teacher, a landscaper, and a cabinet maker, and had never done any woodcarving.

In spite of this, he took his recently gained knowledge, the carving tools his wife gave him for his birthday, and his enthusiasm, and carved his first carousel pony. Then he carved more, working an hour in the morning before his job and after dinner until ten. He took a pony to the mayor of Missoula and told him his dream. The mayor sent him to others who in spite of their initial skepticism were won over by his sincerity and vision. The ponies were placed everywhere people were; raising awareness of the project in storefronts, shopping centers, schools, the county fair, doctors' offices, and parties. Donations began to come in. Mechanics, carvers, and organizers would show up on his doorstep. The carvers worked together in the evenings collaborating on ponies. No one on the project ever accepted a dime for their efforts.

Each pony had a sponsor. And each sponsor had a hand in designing the pony. Schoolchildren raised the funds for "Snapples," a pinto with apples on its bridle and saddle. The Sons of Norway sponsored a Norwegian Fjord Horse. "Orchard Belle" wears a straw hat and blinders and has vegetables behind her saddle. She was created to honor the truck farms that once provided a livelihood for many in the area. There is also a Pony Express horse, an Appaloosa in recognition of the Native American community, and a horse named "Hard Hat," with a saw on its saddle and brickwork on the straps, sponsored by construction workers. The hollow bellies of the horses contain memorabilia placed there by their sponsors and the carousel volunteers.

The carousel now stands in Missoula's Caras Park beside a river. Riding the carousel gives you a thrilling sense of humor, delight, gratitude, heritage, altruism; gifts of a man with a vision and the collaboration of a community. It is living art that creates an awareness of continuity among generations past, present, and future.

Does the artist have to be an individual or can the artist be a community? Can you think of ways a community might be the artist? How can your artwork be an expression of continuity?

Murals are the most common example students think of when considering the artist as a community. We have many murals in Tucson that are largely inspired by the Latino culture, which has always been an integral part of the city and traditionally highly values community. A California artist, Judith Baca, worked with rival gang members to create a mural along the Los Angeles aqueducts that spoke of the heritage of that region and the need for reconciliation. Some of my students have worked with at-risk youths creating murals and a sense of community, in town and on the Tohono O'odham reservation. Other students mention The Dinner Party, envisioned by Judy Chicago, and collaborated on by many women, and also the Names Project Quilt; a collaboration on a national scale, with thousands of participants, that has done much to raise awareness of the AIDS epidemic.

One of my own experiences with creative collaboration occurred when five women artists at our church decided to create a huge, 18'x15', Easter banner for the wall in front of the sanctuary, behind the altar. One of the artists, Anne Sullivan, designed a quilt pattern, partially on the computer, which required approximately 1,800 6"x6" squares of patterned fabric, mostly in floral prints, a few with flying pigs carrying purses. Each square was heat set with an iron onto a background cloth. The design was a complex color composition that gradually and irregularly moved from dark to light, scintillating with pattern and color, flowing upwards, full of life; a symbol of the Easter Resurrection and our individual and communal striving for conversion. At first no one felt they had the time to take on this commitment. Everyone had a dozen other responsibilities; work, family, art careers. However we discovered that the time was there if we wanted it to be and the banner was created, square, by square, by square. After a month of weekends the "quilt" was complete. For years this banner improved the worship environment of 1,500 people each week of the Easter season, and awed visitors. None of the five artists really wanted the project to end. Collaborating and creating something together, that came out of our shared awareness of faith and was made to serve our community, was a rewarding experience.

I often wondered at the quiet intensity of the experience of reflecting on a Zen garden. Then once, when visiting Daitoku-ji in Kyoto, Japan, I watched a worker caring for a garden, shaping a pine tree, needle by needle. He was quietly sitting in the tree, plucking them by hand, focused on the individual tree, its place in the garden, the intent of the community it served. Where the Easter banner took a commitment of a month of collaboration by five individuals, the Zen gardens of Kyoto often represent a collaboration of hundreds of years and many generations. After watching him work for hours, I no longer wondered where the quiet intensity of the garden came from. It was the gift of countless individuals who contributed to the larger truth of the community, creating a living work of art.

When we think of art in the contemporary European tradition, we most often think of individual expression. Our awareness is the celebration of the individual. We tend to think of an artist as an isolated individual somehow above and separate from community. I believe this is limiting and deceiving and leads to much misplaced ego. Since reflecting on the contributions of the artists in this book, and stories like Chuck Kaparich's, I have become much more aware that my art is a gift made possible by all who have gone before me and helped me along the way. In a sense, it is a collaboration with my ancestors who braved everything to come to this country, the relatives who grew up poor, yet through the decisions they made and hard work, gave me many more choices and a college education, my extended and immediate family who create life-giving connections, my teachers who struggled and made sacrifices to share things that matter, my faith community and the communion of saints that is my foundation. It is a privilege to be in a position to make art. It is inextricably bound to a collaboration of generations and potentially holds the promise of a continuous gift of life.

Pineapple Quilt, Atanacia Santa Cruz Hughes. Photo: Arizona Historical
Society/Tucson, AHS#: 84.1.1

Connections

In the United States, quilts are one way families of many backgrounds have strengthened their family ties, reinforced their heritage, felt connected to each other. *Grand Endeavors: Vintage Quilts and Their Makers*, a publication resulting from the Arizona Quilt Project, presents many such quilts and the stories of those who made them.

In 1884, Atanacia Hughes, the wife of a merchant and prominent citizen in the early years of Tucson, made a Pineapple quilt. Atanacia had been raised to possess the skills prized in a refined Mexican lady, including fine embroidery and sewing. Each block in the quilt contains a center square embroidered with religious symbols, flowers, or Spanish words. Within this symbolism is a message to her family. Loosely translated it says "We married at a holy time. We became a faithful family. One key guides us in a straight line" (Frost and Stevenson 1992, 7).

Another remarkable quilt was created by Nellie von Gerichten Smith in the 1900s. Her husband owned the Palace Bar in Prescott. Between 1895 and 1914, she collected hundreds of the tiny blue ribbons that were attached to the necks of Pabst Blue Ribbon beer bottles. She stitched them into a Tumbling Block pattern, creatively using different colored threads to enhance and emphasize different blocks. The result is a whimsical and artistic statement of family history (Frost and Stevenson 1992, 104).

Esther Olds Nichols made a quilt in 1907 that includes blocks with the embroidered outlines of the hands of three generations of family members. She stitched the outlines of the hands of her daughter, son-in-law, and several grandchildren. One block shows two tiny baby hands and the words "Melvin 1907 April 1st." Her own hands show fingers crippled by arthritis. The quilt was made for a small granddaughter and although many of those represented on the quilt have passed away, it continues to connect generations of the Nichols family (Frost and Stevenson 1992, 188).

The early years of Arizona usually meant a lot of hard work and challenge for pioneering women. Quilts tended to be made of bits and pieces of whatever was around, chronicling the life of the maker and her family. Some quilts were made to commemorate a special event, such as a wedding or a birth, others affirm aspects of daily life. "The colorful quilts added a spot of brightness to the women's homes and to their lives. And, unlike most of the daily chores that filled a woman's life, the "work" of making a quilt rewarded her with a tangible creation that could be used, admired, and even passed on to future generations" (Frost and Stevenson 1992, xiii). The quilts of the pioneering women of Arizona are lasting testimonies of these women's commitment to their families and their own creative spirit.

Is there a way of using your creativity that helps you, your family and/or friends connect with each other? Do you own something handmade by a family member or friend?

Reflecting on the first question, many students seem to realize for the first time that using their creativity to connect with family and friends might be a legitimate use of their gifts. Too often we take the commonplace for granted. It is increasingly easy to be distracted by the myriad of choices we have (TV, movies, computer games) that do not directly engage us with other people; leaving us isolated and our creativity essentially unused. Creating something for someone else, or actively creating together, developing a skill, and fostering an aesthetic awareness can be very rewarding and connecting.

Some students do use their creativity to help their family and friends connect with each other and give examples such as handmade gifts and creative memory albums. A former student in her seventies, who has a heart condition and is largely confined to her home, called to tell me how much she was enjoying making paintings about her family's Norwegian heritage and how appreciated they are by the extended family who receive them. Other students spend a lot of time decorating or making aesthetically pleasing feasts for various holidays. Two students, in different classes, had a particularly wonderful creative tradition. They told me that their families all gather at a family member's house for Christmas. No one is allowed in, from the youngest to the eldest, unless they have brought a handmade Christmas tree ornament. They decorate the tree together with all of the ornaments brought throughout the years, producing a creative and joyous shared memory.

Another student told me that for years, out of necessity, she made many things for her family by hand, including clothing, Christmas ornaments, costumes and gifts. Later she had a job and more income. Although her family now had designer jeans and "the latest," she felt much was lost. During this period the handmade ornaments the family had made were inadvertently thrown out. She said it was like losing an old friend. To retrieve the feelings of connection and the satisfaction of being creative that making something personal gives, the family made more ornaments together.

As we increasingly choose the omnipresent and convenient assembly line aesthetic, whether in our dwellings, furnishings, or clothing, it is becoming less common to own objects made by a family member or friend. Also, some art students seem to have bought into the contemporary myth of the entirely self-realized individual and have never considered heritage and family connections to be relevant or of value. However, they begin to see things differently when they listen to their classmates' stories of cherished handmade belongings.

A young student talked about how gratifying it was to live in a house made by his grandfather and feel a grounding connection with someone loved and admired on a daily basis. While he was growing up he learned from his grandfather and he continues to make things by hand himself. Others tell of a piece of handmade furniture they own, an art project proudly presented by a child, a sweater that has become a favorite and a source of great solace, and very often they speak of quilts and afghans. Many a student has related to me how a quilt or afghan was taken out of the closet to comfort someone who was sad or sick.

One memorable quilt story was told by two unrelated students who grew up in the hills of Appalachia and just happened to be in my class at the same time. Their experience was similar. In their words, they grew up "dirt poor." Their mothers would save the strip of cloth that is pulled off the top when opening feed bags and when they had enough strips they would painstakingly sew them into a quilt. The rest of the feed bag was used to make clothing. My students told me those quilts were sacred, a symbol of family unity, and "nobody messed with them."

When I first started teaching, in 1978, I wouldn't allow my weaving students to make baby blankets, as they were not "serious art." They have changed my mind. In recent years many a student has woven a creative, personal baby blanket, with love and anticipation, for an expected niece, nephew or grandchild. Once I showed a weaving class a picture of a "serious artist" who had meticulously lined up thousands of pennies in rows on the floor of a gallery and then sat compulsively washing her hands in an old hat, depicting isolation and neurosis. I asked them what they thought. They said if someone is feeling that much isolation and neurosis, they should get it together and weave a baby blanket, connect with family, connect with community, focus on love, think of someone other than themselves. I thought it was startlingly good advice.

Two artists I deeply admire committed suicide. I respect the intensity of their work and feel I somewhat understand. I know when I am working intensely I struggle to make myself eat, sleep, exercise, connect with those around me. Stretching for the expression of an ideal you can never entirely reach and only partially sense, coupled with physical exhaustion, can easily lead to despair, if a conscious effort is not made to connect with others. Maybe we should all make a "baby blanket" sometime; something like Calder's circus, to share with friends and family.

I once received such a gesture as a New Year's blessing, from an internationally recognized artist, whose work I greatly respect. I had the pleasure of visiting her in her studio, in Kyoto, the year before. She spoke very little English. I spoke next to zero Japanese. Yet we had a wonderful visit; sharing each others' work and enjoying each others' presence. For New Year's, she sent me a three inch square of delicate paper she made herself, that looks and feels close to the earth. In the center is imbedded a blue rectangle (my logo) also of handmade paper. A single golden thread is stitched into the paper and a spot of goldleaf has been pressed into place by a finger. It is exquisitely sensitive. I found it more eloquent and gravid than verbal communication - breath for the soul. I cherish it still.

The connection between hand and spirit is a potent one. When I was going through a difficult time a helpful priest gave me a fairly lengthy relevant prayer he had copied by hand. Moved but amazed, I asked him, "But why didn't you just photocopy it?" Equally amazed he answered, "Because I wanted to copy it by hand." I felt the prayer more deeply, because he had done so.

When we make something by hand for someone else, because of the time-consuming nature of the process, we expose ourselves to prolonged focus on good and life-giving values. When we live with something someone has made for us on a regular basis, we experience gratitude, a sense of continuity, comfort and caring. These are all connections that make it more difficult for the darker side of life to take hold.

Sioux Moccasins ca.1890. Photo: Grand Teton National Park Archives

Resources and Choice

There are numerous practices in Native American cultures that express a respect for creation and a reverent use of its resources. Many examples are found in *Dancing Colors: Paths of Native American Women*, which was compiled by two Native Americans from Plains nations. The book has moving pictures of women from several nations, pictures of their environment, their stories, beliefs, and the objects they made for daily use. It speaks of these women's understanding of the connection of nature, religion, and everyday life. Many Native Americans say that in their culture there is no distinction between art and life. Both are part of a whole.

The designs and colors used on an object are often symbolic. In Plains culture: "Certain designs used in decoration belonged to particular families and were handed down from mother to daughter. The elements of life were represented by a variety of symbols: a cross is a star in the heavens, and a triangle is a mountain or tipi. Colors also have special meaning; white symbolizes age; green is growth and development; yellow represents maturity and perfection; and red is sacred and means life" (Brafford and Thom 1992, 24). The combination of symbols and colors used can tell a story.

Many generations worth of traditions continue to be taught by mothers and grandmothers to their children and grandchildren. Older women are respected for their wisdom and knowledge and continue to be useful to their families and tribes. Beliefs and values are reinforced through the making of objects.

One value that was upheld when making moccasins, was a respect for resources. When taking from the earth and its creatures, prayers were offered. "Although the land was bountiful with buffalo, Plains Indian women reused their old tipis to make clothing. Moccasins were made from smoke flaps of an old tipi, because they had been waterproofed by the smoke" (Brafford and Thom 1992, 72). When the soles of moccasins wore out, the decorated tops were often recycled into drawstring pouches. Resources were not wasted. Objects had purpose; function and often symbolism - partially out of necessity, partially through choice.

Do the objects you surround yourself with reinforce your values? Are there things you could get rid of or replace with something more meaningful? How can you show respect for resources through your artwork?

As with the traditional Plains cultures, in many cultures around the world relatively few objects are owned and, those that people do possess, serve a basic need and/or reinforce shared beliefs and values. Contemporary society has become a culture of great accumulators; taking from wherever in the world we wish, as much as we want, often with very little thought. Too many times we buy whatever is expedient and cheap, regardless of the quality of the materials or the design, without knowing if our purchase was made in a sweatshop or a prison in appalling circumstances. Instead of buying something that reflects lasting values, we opt for the latest fad or fashion trend. More often than not the expedient, the cheap, the faddish or fashionable ends up discarded and becomes landfill in a very short period of time. Rarely do we make purchases that consciously reflect and reinforce lasting values, including the wise use of resources. To do this we might need to save money for a time, make one carefully thought-out researched purchase, and avoid surrounding ourselves with basically thoughtless clutter. Perhaps we can choose something made by hand that embodies values that give life or instead of being the ultimate consumers, slow down on occasion and make what we need with thought and care; something that can be used and appreciated for generations.

The house of the Japanese ceramic artist and philosopher, Kanjiro Kawai, impresses me deeply. It is now a museum in Kyoto, Japan, and I spent a rainy morning there, padding around in my stocking feet, allowed to explore at will. Everything is pared down to just those surroundings that supported his beliefs, values, and life work. The living quarters are all of wood and along with the sparse furnishings, were carefully crafted by traditional Japanese folk artists, whose values he deeply respected. There are also some wood sculptures he made himself. All rooms in the house have sliding paper shoji screens that, when opened, allow unfettered air and look upon a central garden, providing a quiet focus. There is a library of beautiful books he collected for inspiration that visitors are invited to leaf through. A corridor is a gallery of his work. The work space where he made his ceramics contains a simple and reverent shrine. His potter's wheel is imbedded in a bench of hand-crafted wood and is placed adjacent to a shoji screen so that he could gaze upon the garden when he worked. His low-fire kiln and climbing kiln are adorned with visual prayers made of paper and straw. A very small room, where he wrote, faces yet another view of the garden. It contains a beautifully crafted, well cared for, writing table to kneel at and a humble charcoal brazier, on a floor of tatami mat. A pen and a ceramic vase with a single flower in it are on the table. And that is all. It is a place of focus and integrity. Slowly I am trying to make decisions that bring more of this into my own life.

I believe Kanjiro Kawai's house is an example of how an artist can respectfully use resources. It is pared down to essentials, reflects and reinforces his beliefs and values, supports his life work. It is filled with objects of integrity; objects that are true to the deepest convictions of those who made them and those who own them. His home is created with quality craftsmanship and materials. It is made by hand and made to last.

So often in our culture the importance of the visual is commercial or trivialized. It is either used to sell superficial ideas or considered spiritually suspect and of little significance. Yet if we pay attention to the objects we surround ourselves with, we will see that they can have an enormously positive impact; helping us to live our beliefs and values. I bring to class a sake set I purchased in Japan that I keep in my living room. It exhibits a great sensitivity to shape and glaze. It is a beautiful matte grey on the outside, which glows with a subtle luster, and has a refined yet earthen texture, calming to the touch. On the inside of the cups is a cool, resonant, green glaze; refreshing in its quiet variations. I explain that my guests never belt down sake when using it. Instead guests assume the sense of serenity and acute perception the artist put into his work. It is a gift the artist gives to us every time we use the sake set he made; helping us to live as artists. Clay and glaze become support for our best intentions; an object of integrity for maker and user, a respectful use of resources.

As with the moccasins, respectfully using resources also involves how we use materials when making art. I like to think about the Zen discipline of "make the living use of a thing." An example, given by a Zen master, is to empty a washbasin around a tree needing water instead of just dumping it (Suzuki 1934, 54). The artist Gyöngy Laky creates sculpture and "drawings" from tree prunings she gathers from orchardists in Northern California. My first very influential teacher, Neda Alhilali, once did a series of wall size art works that looked liked constructions made of enormous colored feathers. They were actually recycled cans; tin-snipped, filed, painted and riveted together. She had a studio near the Los Angeles airport and the transients in the neighborhood knew that at a certain time each week they could sell her cans. She recycled and transformed trash into something extraordinary and beautiful and helped sustain those who hadn't any sustenance. Neda made the choice to make the "living use of the thing."

Being an artist does not involve just the act of creation, it is all of life: what we surround ourselves with, our focus, our choices. At the end of each semester I show my students a moon mask, hand-carved from a piece of alder wood by an artist named Dennis Leon, who is a member of the Salish nation and who lives on the northwest coast of Canada. Mask making is not a part of the Salish tradition, but there is a rich heritage of mask making by many Native American nations indigenous to this region and this inspired him to try his hand. He does so masterfully. The strong and benevolent face that emerges from the wood, follows the grain in a graceful marriage of image and material. The surface is unpainted except for a few highlights in red and black around the eyes and the wood has been reverently finished so that it has a deep, quiet radiance. Although I have never met the artist, I believe he could not have made such a sensitive unified form without limiting his choices, honing his focus.

Choice is something we Americans are blessed with in over abundance, giving us immense responsibility. Not long ago, my brother told me about a conversation he had with a woman who counsels recent immigrants who are having trouble adjusting to the United States. One of the most difficult adjustments many immigrants must make is dealing with the overwhelming number of choices, some would say "freedoms," we are privileged to have.

This abundance is apparent in all manner of life decisions from the ability to choose a career, or change careers at any age (unlike many countries where your "aptitudes" are tested and "determined" at an early age, you are channeled into a profession, and due to many circumstances, economic and social, that is essentially that) to everyday choices, such as the five-page menus we often encounter or the decisions involved in ordering something as simple as a pizza. For example, you may be asked to contemplate the relative merits of mozzarella, provolone, cheddar, feta, Romano, Swiss, ricotta, Parmesan, or soy alternative; to cogitate on the choice of pepperoni, Italian sausage, capicolla, Canadian bacon, oven roasted chicken, ground beef, salami, bacon, or anchovies; and to wrestle with the determination of whether you want artichokes, fresh mushrooms, yellow or red onions, fresh green bell peppers, fresh tomatoes, jalapenos, roasted green chilies, green olives, roasted red peppers, fresh yellow squash, scallions, broccoli, roasted eggplant, pepperoncinis, sun-dried tomatoes, fresh spinach or zucchini. And then there are the mega-stores you need to wear hiking boots to in order to comfortably negotiate the miles of aisles lined with choices.

The counselor recommends to the immigrants that whether they are in a restaurant or contemplating a career, they should carefully limit their choices before they engage in the actual situation. They should then stick to these limitations for a designated time before they re-evaluate: choice control.

Immigrants are not alone in the dilemma of a plethora of choices. I have chosen to live my life as an artist and thanks to the artists in this book I am increasingly aware of how so many other of my decisions affect my life, affect my art. Blessed with an abundance of resources and opportunities, I pray that my choices will engender the wisdom I need to make still better ones. I wonder what it would be like to further pare down the trappings of my existence and surround myself with a bare minimum of objects of integrity. And know that I have sometimes allowed myself to get lost in possibilities instead of choosing for myself a situation and a focus that creates true freedom and fulfillment through limitation, through values that matter; like a sacramental marriage or the home and life of an artist, such as Kanjiro Kawai.

Old Glory/Shroud#1 by James Bassler. Photo: James Bassler

Craftsmanship

A video I show on Kyoto joinery presents traditional Japanese woodworkers engaged in their craft. Kyoto woodworkers first settled near large Buddhist temples to make objects used in ceremonies. Later they also worked for the samurai class and wealthy merchants. In the video they are making objects used for the tea ceremony and tea rooms. The craftsmen aim for simplicity of design, attention to detail, refined execution, a product that is pleasing to the eye and touch.

The wood that is used is often cured for thirty years. What is cut today will be used by the woodworkers of the next generation. The boards from a single tree are kept together and placed in the order they are cut, so that the grain will be used in a way that is harmonious in the final product. The wood is cut by hand, paying attention to the grain and wasting as little as possible. One woodworker said, "The wood is a living thing. So it is cruel to the wood itself if you make a mistake" (Diamond, Inc. 1992).

The craftsmen work in silence, using hand tools. The tools are simple. The skill is in the craftsman. Their tools are treated reverently, honed daily, beautifully made, and passed on from generation to generation. The woodworkers make joints carefully without any nails. The strength of the joint is in the craftsmanship; the way it is designed, cut, planed, to a hundredth of an inch. The "hell joint" consists of a piece of wood that is slit several times on one end so that it fans out a little. It is placed in a hole in another piece of wood designed so that it can just fit in. Then the fan spreads inside the hole so that it can never get out again. Rice paste is used as glue and, because the joints are well crafted, this is enough. The craftsman makes the paste himself and carefully controls the consistency.

One woodworker is making a small cabinet. He shows how he cut by hand the grooves in the side panels, in which the drawers slide back and forth. In the front the groove is 3.04 inches, in the back it is 3.07 inches. This allows the air to escape when the drawer is being moved in and out, but the cabinet is virtually air-tight. Another woodworker makes a frame for a floor hearth. He sews a thin strip of cherry bark through the wood for detail and his finishing is impeccable, even though most of this will never show once the frame is in place. These objects are made to last two hundred to three hundred years. "We work the wood gently so it will last that long...The work has to be invisible" (Diamond, Inc. 1992).

Finishing is done entirely with natural materials, applied directly by hand. A block with a bottom layer consisting of horsetail plant is used as a gentle abrasive for the first finishing. It won't scratch the surface of the wood and contains a small amount of oil to lubricate and polish. Next mulberry leaves are rubbed against the wood's surface. The backs of mulberry leaves have minute barbs. The final polish is the secretions of caterpillars that live on the wax tree. With the heat of the hand the waxy secretions melt into the surface of the wood, protecting it from being soiled and preserving its natural beauty.

This process is reflected in the finished product and the craftsmen themselves.

> Do not make light of the trivial deeds of daily life, for great virtues are born of them (Suzuki 1934, 153).

What ideas and values are evident in this example of craftsmanship? What is the role of craftsmanship in contemporary art?

There is a prevailing view in the contemporary art world that craftsmanship is of very little or no importance. What is considered important is the visual expression of ideas. What is being missed by this way of thinking is how many important ideas are expressed through craftsmanship.

The objects the woodworkers make reflect the values these craftsmen have brought to the process. We see Patience: the wood is cured for thirty years, skills are developed over a long period of time, the process is never rushed. Integrity: the care evident in the part of the object the viewer sees is also taken where it will never be seen. Reverence: the objects allow the natural beauty of the wood to prevail. Harmony is seen in their sensitivity to the grain of the wood. Simplicity is apparent in the unembellished designs. Respect for resources: care is taken to avoid all waste and only small amounts of natural materials are used. Continuity: an awareness of generations and timelessness is evident throughout the process, in the curing of the wood, the maintenance of the tools, the appreciation of the objects lasting three hundred years. Reflection: the process is meditative, great care is taken in every step. The cacophony and speed of power tools are not present. Humility: the objects purpose and the principles of Tea, sometimes expressed as harmony, respect, purity, and tranquility, are the focus of the process and infused in the craftsmanship (Urasenke Foundation, 1993). The craftsman keeps his own ego in check.

Attention to craftsmanship can also give powerful expression to ideas in contemporary art. I have seen many artists attempt to express their discontent with the policies of the United States through a manipulation of the image of the American flag. These attempts have often appeared slammed together and ill-considered. A common claim of contemporary artists is that any reaction from the viewer justifies their art's existence. Yet slammed together artistic statements can encourage equally ill-considered reactions. Not much that is positive results. My experience was very different when I encountered James Bassler's hand-woven American flag titled "Old Glory," displayed with "Shroud#1."

"Old Glory" is a wall-size American flag, 72"x 126", painstakingly hand-woven in wedge-weave and then blotched by the artist with black dye in a way that reveals large stenciled letters spelling "SOILED," with the word "OIL" emphasized. Below it lies a carefully woven body bag. The colors, pattern and technique he uses subtly suggest his appreciation of and sense of connection with the cultures of Central and South America, Africa and the Dine. The opening along the shroud's top is also painted with a black dye implying sorrow and defilement. Bassler says this work grew from his outrage at some of our country's policies. His anguish is powerfully expressed. The success of his statement is partially a result of the time and care put into the process, his craftsmanship. To defile a flag that was lovingly made through hundreds of hours of work, careful decisions and reflection, speaks to us of a deep and honest commitment. The beauty of the craftsmanship in the flag and the shroud also speak of a love of country and an empathy for other people, that give power to the pain and a sense of underlying hope. There is love, hope, and commitment in this work that might otherwise be despairing. The conscientious craftsmanship allows us to experience them. I first saw this work in an exhibit in a rural town. The curator told me the museum's patrons tended to be conservative and she was surprised when she did not receive complaints about this piece. Perhaps this was because the care taken in making "Old Glory/Shroud #1" is evident and invites reflection, rather than knee-jerk reaction. And reflection is more likely to lead to a true conversion of ideas.

When I see a disregard of craftsmanship, I also see ideas expressed. I often see arrogance. I see a disrespect of resources and an impatience that fosters ill-considered ideas that do more harm than good. Students from less privileged circumstances and less developed countries have told me that what I call the "art of despair," devoid of craftsmanship and focusing on what is wrong with the world without hope, could only be made by those who are spoiled. When you grow up in difficult circumstances, you know how important it is to focus on and hold onto what brings life. It is your salvation.

Oval Boxes in the Shaker Style by Paul Dixon, Orleans Carpenters.
Photo: Mingei International Museum

Time

Kindred Spirits: The Eloquence of Function in American Shaker and Japanese Arts of Daily Life is the catalog of the exhibition of the same name, shown at the Mingei International Museum in San Diego in 1995. The beautiful Shaker and Japanese objects presented in the catalog speak of common values, although they arose from very different circumstances. The Shakers were at their height in the late 1700s and in the 1800s as a communal, celibate, Protestant, monastic society composed of men and women in the United States. The Japanese objects are derived from an aesthetic that grew from many aspects of the culture of a nation, notably indigenous Shinto beliefs with an emphasis on purity. Both the Shaker and Japanese creations represented in the catalog emanate a sense of simplicity, humility, dignity, and reverence.

In the essays of the catalog there are some thought-provoking perceptions on awareness of time:

From the Shakers: "Do your work as though you had a thousand years to live, and as if you were to die tomorrow...Put your hands to work and your hearts to God, and a blessing will attend you" (Sprigg: Mingei International 1995, 11).

Dr. Soetsu Yanagi, the great advocate of Japanese folk art, "... recognized that unsurpassed beauty was the flowering of a unified expression when there is no division of head, heart and hands and that, with the increasing mechanization of society, few people perform an act of total attention" (Longenecker: Mingei International 1995, 16).

What does an act of total attention mean to you? How do you experience time when you create? Do you equate time with money?

Some years ago a school administrator said to me, "We must find faster, more efficient ways to teach. The pace of life is getting faster. Our students' attention spans are getting shorter. We must find ways to use the new technology to speed things up." I ask, why is the answer to speed up? For me the answers come when I slow down.

I make a point of giving a long involved project in each of my classes; a project that is at least a month in duration, that can not be solved all at once, and requires reflection, evolution, growth. At first there is often some resistance, but in the end most students are grateful. By slowing down, they are able to pull out of themselves an excellence and a peace of mind they did not even know was there. Not long ago, a former student stopped me in the grocery store and told me that working on the extended project was one of the peak experiences of his life. This tells me we need more such opportunities in contemporary life.

Another student I had many years ago said to me, "When I took your class I was going through a divorce. I was not seeking answers when I sat down to work on my art projects, but when I slowed down and allowed the process to take over, the answers were there." Time to reflect is absolutely essential to our mental and physical well-being. Time, discipline, hard work, discernment allow our experiences to become fully integrated with our souls. Without reflection, our experiences do not give direction to our lives and merely flit about like the images of an MTV video. Time to reflect seems less and less valued by popular culture.

The rewards of a slow creative process can also be seen in the ordinary actions of our daily lives. One of my favorite stories was told to me by a Dine (Navajo) student. This student grew up on the reservation in northern Arizona; a place of vast, uncluttered horizons. When she told me this story, she resided in Tucson. She was a full-time student, a costume designer, she had her own theater company and a family. She felt fractured and often came to class exhausted. When she goes to visit her mother on the reservation, her mother says to her, "You are out of balance. Let's spend the day making bread the old way." My student protests and offers to go and buy bread at the store. But her mother insists and eventually prevails. Mother and daughter spend the day outside together, grinding the ingredients, mixing them, and then baking and tending the bread in the traditional outdoor oven. My student says, she has to admit her mother is right. She always feels much better afterward. I told this story during a lecture in New Jersey, and an artist in the audience said she understood. One day she was feeling sick from the emotional strain of a recent divorce. She called her sister and her sister told her to pick herself up, go down to the kitchen and make soup from scratch. She did and it helped.

Have you ever noticed how incredibly beautiful a slice of carrot is? The structure of celery? The color of beets? We have to slow down and focus to do so. At one time I created a series of art works, in which each piece featured a rock and was made with the coiling technique, a traditional basketry process. I prayed before I worked. I thought about what it might mean to work as if I had a thousand years to live and as if I were to die tomorrow. The coiling process is very time consuming. I frequently managed only three inches of coiling an hour in a single row.

The reward came from slowing down. I was often awestruck by the unimaginable beauty of the very ordinary rock I found in my front yard; a small piece of creation, a window to the timeless. The peace and wholeness I experienced was a wondrous gift.

The joy of an act of total attention is a big reason many of us choose art. Our increasingly complex world provides us with more and more choices; more and more distractions. Mechanization has brought us many rewards. But it can also lead us to think in terms of dollars per hour, and that an efficient use of our time means increased production. This is at odds with the art process. An act of total attention requires an indifference to time, a focus leading to a unity of hands, heart and mind rather than production. So much stuff, so little quality. The technology of the information age has multiplied our choices many times over. Nearly everyone I speak to feels increasingly fractured, pulled in too many directions, time crunched. As our choices increase, it is easier and easier to be distracted from what is important to us. Yet for the most part it is in our hands; it is our choice.

A former student of mine recently became homeless, because of difficulties caused by multiple chemical sensitivities. She is living out of her car in the campground of a local mountain retreat to escape the conditions that cause her serious physical reactions. We are both actively trying to find ways to improve her circumstances and she comes to visit me every few weeks. When she comes she also shares with me the merits of just slowing down. She brings me sticks with complex pathways made by insects and wonders at their map-like quality, tiny metropolises. She gave me a rock that is "like a puzzle," with pieces that fit seamlessly. When you remove them, underneath is more fathomless beauty. She speaks of being able to see the stars at night unfettered in their brilliance and infinite numbers by city lights. We give thanks for what I call "just seeing" and for "just being." Our visits are joyous. I admire her spirit greatly.

I like to think about my Dine student baking bread outdoors with her mother. I am happy to know that an ordinary rock found in my front yard has awesome truths to share when I slow down enough to reflect, through creating a work of art. I am thankful that a way of experiencing, a slow and focused creative process helps to instill, can assist in sustaining a talented young woman in difficult circumstances.

It leads me to consider the advice a sage gave a Moroccan student, when the student went to him in the desert. "Focus on just one thing. Just one thing." An act of total attention is a timeless gift art has to give.

Sacred Grass by Gloria Petyarre. Photo: Utopia Art Sydney & Gloria Petyarre

Cross-cultural Inspiration

The Art of Utopia: A New Direction in Contemporary Aboriginal Art contains a striking collection of art works by Aboriginal artists from a community in central Australia named Utopia.

In their struggle to remain autonomous, members of the community were introduced to acrylic paint and canvas as a means of support and a way to raise awareness of their unique cultural heritage.

Many of the most powerful paintings are inspired directly by Aboriginal beliefs about what is often referred to as "Dreaming." Dreaming is a complex belief system involving ritual and ceremonies, the landscape itself, and a sense of time described as no time and all time. Different members of a group are responsible for specific living stories for a particular Dreaming.

The Anangu Aboriginal people of the Uluru or Ayers Rock region had the most continuous culture on earth, estimated at 35,000 to 75,000 years, until the arrival of Europeans about 200 years ago. They explain Dreaming as follows:

> Tjukurpa is the foundation of our culture.
>
> Some people try to translate Tjukurpa (pronounced like 'chook-orr-pa') as 'Dreaming' or 'Dreamtime'. This does not seem right to us - Tjukurpa is real, not imaginary or fleeting.
>
> Tjukurpa tells of all relationships between people, plants, animals and the physical features of the land.
>
> Tjukurpa refers to the past, present and the future at the same time. It refers to the time Tyukuriitja (ancestral beings), created the world as we know it. Tjukurpa also refers to Anangu religion, law, relationships and moral systems. Anangu life today revolves around Tjukurpa (Australian Government 2006, 18).

The artist Gloria Petyarre uses linear patterns surrounded by dots to create her work titled "Sacred Grass." This painting is inspired by native grasses, ceremonial body painting and a Dreaming she is responsible for. "Sacred Grass" suggests microcosm and macrocosm simultaneously and emanates a sense of the numinous. Another impressive work using imagery inspired by ceremonial designs is a painting composed of six 55"x 28" panels, titled "Ilbanda." Ilbanda means the Bush Plum Dreaming. It was painted by the custodians of the Bush Plum Dreaming: Paddy Jungala, Engarlarka, and Lindsay Bird. "Ilbanda" strongly evokes a sense of the eternal in the present. The content of these paintings is universal and yet deeply rooted in a distinctly Aboriginal heritage.

What challenges do we face as the art of all cultures becomes accessible? Do we have responsibilities as consumers of art? How can we be inspired by the artistic traditions of other cultures, yet still be honest to our own and respectful of theirs?

Our global awareness is increasing at an exceedingly rapid rate. I am amazed at how much more information there is on artists from extremely varied cultures in just the last thirty five years. In 1971, I was in one of the first African Art classes offered at the college level. Information was scarce and most of the books we used were anthropological. I did my senior thesis on West African textiles and it was very difficult to find any references. I would search for bits of information in musty old travel logs by adventurers who just happened to mention textiles they had seen. This was all that was readily accessible for an entire continent. However, this began to change rapidly. In the spring of 1973, the Metropolitan Museum of Art mounted the first major exhibit of African art titled "African Textiles and Decorative Arts." It was accompanied by an extensive catalog. This saved my thesis. Some years later in 1978, I decided to investigate Moroccan Berber textiles. I could find only one recently published article in English and a number of reports in French written by officials during the French protectorate. So I did hands-on research in the United States, London, Paris, and Morocco and eventually consulted for the first major exhibition of Moroccan textiles in the United States, "From the Far West: Carpets and Textiles of Morocco," at the Textile Museum in Washington, D.C., in 1980. Now there are considerable resources on both these subjects. There are exhibitions and beautiful picture books, such as *The Art of Utopia*, on the art of cultures from all over the world. One of the great challenges of our time is what do we do with all of this cultural exchange? Do we turn our new knowledge into yet another commercial endeavor, taking what has meaning to others and rendering it essentially meaningless? Do we use sacred symbols irreverently, without understanding? Or do we focus on what is important to all of us and learn from and support each other?

In 1999 there was a new exhibition of African textiles that addressed these issues: "Wrapped in Pride: Ghanaian Kente and African American Identity" at the U.C.L.A. Fowler Museum. The exhibit did not focus solely on the beauty of the weavings. It emphasized their traditional cultural significance in Asante culture as a symbol of pride, community and dignity, worn and used at all important ceremonies; including the installation of a new chief, festival processions, christenings, weddings and funerals. The exhibit also addressed how kente cloth has been transformed into a symbol of African American dignity and heritage. In an inspiring project, organized by education director Betsy Quick, eighteen Crenshaw High School students spent a year researching the uses of kente in their community. They found it was used for pastors' stoles, clothing and decorations for weddings and for Kwanzaa, tablecloths for special occasions, dolls, everyday clothing, baseball caps, umbrellas, Valentine's Day balloons, Band-Aids, and more. The students' research and a display of examples were incorporated into the exhibition.

This is an intriguing example of the complexity of the issue of appropriation and our responsibility as artists and consumers. As bell hooks states in *Art on My Mind: Visual Politics*, "acts of appropriation are part of the process by which we make ourselves. Appropriating - taking something for one's own use - need not be synonymous with exploitation. This is especially true of cultural appropriation. The 'use' one makes of what is appropriated is the crucial factor" (Ross 1998, 285). Is it the use? It is exciting to see a tradition of textiles created to inspire dignity and reinforce a sense of community do just that, in a new context, on a different continent, for a related people. But at what point does kente's symbolic significance suffer and become outweighed by commercial concerns? Do kente Band-Aids bring comfort through an awareness of community or make kente so common that its symbolic dignity is diminished? I suppose the appropriateness of appropriation is as much in the awareness of the user as the use.

We see the appropriation of symbols everywhere. Years ago, when my daughter was younger, the ying yang symbol was seemingly ubiquitous, and on every imaginable do-dad made for children. Conveniently round like "happy face," the yellow dot with eyes and the black and white paisleys shared the limelight on everything from lunch boxes to necklaces and yes, Band-Aids. My daughter wanted some happy face, ying yang barrettes and I explained to her that the ying yang was an important, meaningful, symbol to some people and we should respect this by forgoing the purchase. To experience reverence we must make choices that bring it into our lives and the lives of others. "A symbol claims human attention and consciousness with a power that seems to be adversely affected by overdose" (Bishops' Committee 1977, 334). This was written as advice on how to assist in creating a visual experience of a sacred space and liturgy, but it applies to our daily decisions as well, whether it is a purchase or a creative determination made by an artist. If we limit our use of a symbol that inspires us, if we use it with care and understanding, rather than losing our freedom of choice, we exercise choice in a way that brings us true freedom; an intensified experience of values that matter such as dignity, community, and reverence. The symbols become "living art," art that brings life. The issues of cross-cultural inspiration are complex, yet worth reflecting on when we make choices and when we create.

Because I teach in the Southwest, the most common instance of appropriation that arises in my classes is a student's desire to use Native American imagery in his or her work. This is done in all innocence, but understandably sometimes makes my Native American students very uncomfortable. Many of my Native American students have grown up in more homogeneous cultural situations, where those they have contact with tend to believe similarly and the distractions of living these beliefs on a daily basis are fewer, than in our more diverse urban American culture. Consequently sacred symbols have retained an intensity that is lost when they are scattered to the winds of appropriation and the cacophony of our commercial environment. Art, belief, and community are an integrated whole. Sacred symbols are often part of everyday life: an ear of corn or a mountain on ancestral lands. When non-Native students come to me and say they want to weave a Navajo blanket, or paint a Kachina, I ask them to consider the significance of those objects to the people who made them. I tell them to learn from the technique, the use of materials, the designs, and most importantly the lessons they teach about community and belief, but then take this knowledge and apply it to express what is most sacred in their own lives. Sometimes they understand and their work is a revelation.

At the end of the semester, when the grades have already been given, occasionally students give me amazing gifts; tangible symbols of what we have shared together. They are treasured by me and help me to carry on. I will share two of them with you. A middle-aged student who had recently retired from working for a phone company for many years, came to my class to pursue her lifelong dream of creating art. Racially she is what we call "black" in this country, but she had been adopted and raised by a "white" family. This had been a struggle for her. She gave me her first precious bowl she had made in her ceramics class. It was a little rough and wobbly, with a lucid green glaze on the outside that looked somewhat Japanese. Inside you see a glowing copper circle on the bottom. When she gave it to me, she was radiant. She told me it was a symbol of coming full circle, personally, racially, cosmologically - a whole. It sits on my desk still. Whenever I see it I think of her beauty and I feel whole. I also have a card a student made for me that speaks of a connectedness to the natural world that is part of his Native American heritage. Time, care, integrity, a sense of the infinite are given breath in the symbol he painted on the front with bold colors, texture, and gesture: a circle. Inside is a blessing:

> Deep Peace of the Running Wave to You.
> Deep Peace of the Flowing Air to You.
> Deep Peace of the Quiet Earth to You.
> Deep Peace of the Shining Stars to You.
> Deep Peace of the Son of Peace to You.
> Deep Peace of the Quintessential Soul to You.

This is a traditional Irish blessing. I am thankful that these students, and many others, had the courage and will to share in this way.

In this modern world, coming together as a whole is inevitable whether we wish for it or not. Painting on canvas is something the Aborigines learned from European culture, but work such as Ilbanda that speaks eloquently, with a powerful intensity, comes from the soul of the artist and is honest to his experience. I hope that we will keep our diversity with strength and clarity as we continue to challenge and teach one another. I pray that we will remind each other about what is important and hold on together.

Hiroshima Kazuo. Photo: Louise Allison Cort

Focus and Strength

Hiroshima Kazuo has been a basketmaker for many years, in the rural mountainous region of Hinokage, on the Japanese island of Kyushu. His chosen profession was partially a result of a dislocated hip he suffered when he was three, in 1917. At that time, in this region, he could not receive the medical attention he needed for this injury. Hiroshima has walked with a limp ever since. School was a long walk from his home. Because of the difficult mountainous terrain, both school and later the most common profession of the region, farming, were not options for him. One of his early memories, from when he was about six, was of a local basketmaker named Mr. Sato. As he worked, Mr. Sato entertained children who gathered around him, by telling fables and myths and crafting bamboo toys. With the encouragement of his parents, at the age of fifteen, Hiroshima Kazuo apprenticed himself to a basketmaker. He completed his apprenticeship two years later and spent a third year in the home of his teacher, working to reimburse him for room and board. In 1933 Hiroshima returned home and lived the life of an itinerant basketmaker. He spent months traveling from one neighboring area to the next, sleeping and eating with each household for about a week while he filled their basket orders. He always worked outside. In the summer he worked twelve to fourteen hours a day, in the winter ten hours a day. For a while, during the war, he taught basketmaking to disabled men. The war brought many changes, making his old life impossible. Beginning in 1947, when he was thirty-two, he stayed in one area and customers brought their orders to him.

Traditionally baskets were an integral part of many aspects of life in the Hinokage region. Hiroshima Kazuo made baskets for numerous cooking functions, such as noodle scoops, soy sauce filters, colanders and trays. Baskets were used in all aspects of farming: cultivating, harvesting, and processing. Hiroshima made ten graded sizes of sieves used for sorting shitake mushrooms. He made many sieves of different designs for different purposes. He made sieves for chaff, crushed corn kernel, tea, bean-paste, and charcoal. Each one is beautiful in its simplicity and integrity of design. Hiroshima crafted backpack baskets to carry heavy loads, such as crops and manure, over the mountainous terrain. He made cylindrical eel traps and baskets to place the eels in once they were caught. Some baskets would last decades, others may be damaged or lost after the first use; yet all were given his complete focus and best craftsmanship.

Hiroshima Kazuo once met a basketmaker named Ushi-don. "I cannot forget that Ushi-don. The wish to be like him - to possess his skill - is with me still." Louise Allison Cort and Kenji Nakamura write in *A Basketmaker in Rural Japan*, "Mr. Hiroshima carries on Ushi-don's creed of not scrimping on the details of even the simplest basket - such as the eel trap that inevitably gets washed away in the river currents. He can recognize where a basketmaker cheated on the details, and he considers such baskets 'fakes'" (Cort and Nakamura 1994, 37). Hiroshima Kazuo selects his materials very conscientiously. Often only a few bamboo stalks can be used in a large stand of bamboo. He prepares his materials with great care and says, "Bamboo is honest - it shows everything" (Cort and Nakamura 1994, 46).

> Making a good basket is not a process of thinking about what to do. It's more like a form of prayer. When I'm working I keep telling myself, 'Do it well, do it well.' I want to make something that will please the person who uses it and suit that person's needs. And I just try to do the work that I can be satisfied with (Cort and Nakamura 1994, 66).

When you spend a great deal of time and effort on a class exercise, a creative project, or something that may not last for long, are you wasting your time? Why? Why not? What is "strong" art to you?

A class exercise that frequently arises in our class discussions of these questions is the notorious grey scale, the first exercise of the semester in my color classes. We spend two weeks and many hours inside and outside of class on grey scales. In its completed state, our grey scale consists of nine painted chips, placed end to end, with equal increments of value (lightness or darkness) between them. The technical purpose of a grey scale is to train a student so that they can distinguish visually and control with their paints minute differences in value, thereby gaining a strong internal sensitivity to value. Yet the process can serve a great deal more than technique and an understanding of value. Some students focus only on the end result and try to get it done as quickly as possible. When they discover it can't be done well in a hurry, they sometimes approach the project hostilely, compounding the problem. After discussions, others will consciously approach the process with patience and discipline, pacing themselves, which most often results in excellence and, to their surprise, enjoyment of the process itself. This excellence and peace of mind spill over into other aspects of their lives and in the quality of their work for the rest of the semester. The virtues of their focus manifest in a very real way.

One of my artist friends told me that when she was in graduate school, she and the other graduates were encouraged to pull out from themselves their most "gut-wrenching experiences" and use those as the focus of their work. One student took the advice literally and created for his thesis exhibition a bucket of vomit and a splattered bathroom wall, inspired by his reaction to his first homosexual experience. Another student depicted death through a completely emaciated figure made of transparent pig-gut hanging from the ceiling in a room with a single glaring lightbulb. I understand these graduate students' dilemma. There is a current maxim, prevalent in the art world, that work does not have "strength" unless it is despairing. Yet there are other ways than despair to experience sex or death. I personally believe despair is over-rated as subject matter and is not something mentors should encourage students to dwell upon, elevate, and flaunt. The singer Jewel once said, "…despairing is basically joining what you abhor" (Newsweek Nov. 23, 1998, 73). How much better to encourage students to ask themselves difficult questions early in their careers that help them to discover what is truly important and significant in their own experience. Too often art students are guided toward fitting into art history, rather than given an opportunity to create art history by developing and exercising their own integrity; in the way such artists as Georgia O'Keeffe have, or the contemporary painter Hope Neill.

In her series of paintings that comprise "A Continual Dreaming," Hope Neill chooses strength over despair, honors her Aboriginal community and serves humanity. The series is composed of several sections. The first set of paintings very directly reflects her community's heritage and spirituality. She writes, "Although my own traditional way of life has drastically changed since the arrival of the Europeans, my innate Aboriginal values have altered little. The Dreaming always was, and will always be a continuum of a state of being." She then moves to paintings that express the sorrow and hardships of Aboriginal people forcibly removed from ancestral lands and placed on reserves - of Aboriginal children wrenched from their parents and placed in missions. Hope's own father was such a child and Hope grew up on a mission where her parents over-saw a dormitory. This aspect of the Australian Aboriginal experience is truly "gut-wrenching," yet throughout the exhibition her message is one of hope; founded in her people's spiritual and communal heritage, their children and future. The final painting is an image of reconciliation with both Aboriginal and Christian imagery and the series' objectives are stated in the accompanying catalog as being: "An Acceptance of Our History; To share with all Australians and indeed all people the truth within our history and culture - To express our philosophy of learning, caring and sharing to all people - To unite all people to work towards a common goal of equity and social justice." Hope donates all profits from the sales and reproductions of this body of work to a Trust which supports Aboriginal spiritual and cultural practices in health, the arts, and education. Through her art, Hope Neill has united diverse cultural and artistic influences into a statement of great integrity (Neill 1993).

There is strength in integrity and strength in facing difficult issues, in a manner that gives life and doesn't compound the problem with more emptiness - for the artist and for the viewer. It is more demanding and rewarding to search the heart than the gut, to temper and nourish the soul. Rembrandt endured the untimely deaths of many members of his immediate family; yet when he painted death, he painted light. Hope Neill faces a cultural burden with grace. Hiroshima Kazuo knew adversity throughout his life, yet he chose to humbly serve.

My students also make such choices. A student of mine is an exhibiting artist, lives with two grown children who suffer from severe depression, and works two jobs to support her son's partner who is dying of AIDS. She told me that thinking about the importance of our focus during the creative process and the potential of this awareness, changed her whole experience of art-making and continues to bring her peace and fulfillment. Her patience and determination are evident in the way she creates and the way she lives.

What we choose to give to the world through our art remains with those who experience it. How we focus and what we focus on during all those hours of creating remains within us; becomes a part of who we are, and influences the other aspects of our lives, whether our work continues to exist or not. Our choices are the pebbles thrown into still waters; the ripple effect in action. The well made eel trap has a lasting effect even if the currents claim it the first time it is used.

We see the same simplicity, patience, fortitude, integrity, dignity, and humility in Hiroshima Kazuo's baskets, that we see in the story of his life. Like the bamboo they are woven from, both the man and his work are honest and serve humankind. The choices Kazuo makes in his life, his focus, are reflected in his work and in him.

There is a quote I am very fond of from a film that is partially about Islamic craftsmen. Near the end of the film it shows a man who makes haircombs from wood in his shop, that is so small it looks like a cupboard in a wall and has a floor about five feet square. It is in one of the old cities, or "medinas," of Morocco. He sits on the floor, bending over a comb he is working on, sawing the teeth of the comb, one by one, by hand, propping his work with his feet so that his whole body is engaged. He says that as he works he focuses on Allah, and his countenance and smile are full of light. The quote is as follows: "In a technological society, the skill is in the machine with very little in the man. In a society of craftsmen the skill is in the man with very little in his tools. So, in a sense, as you perfect the skills, you also perfect the man" (Cross, 1976).

When we work on a class exercise, a basket, or a painting, whether we are wasting our time or creating something of eternal value is up to us. It depends on how we define strength, our resolve and our focus.

Kanchipuram Woman. Photo: Stephen P. Huyler

Process and Faith

A workworn hand covered in mud resurfaces a dirt wall. A much used bowl filled with a mixture of ochre and water, with a brush made of grass resting in it, waits to be used. Hindu women on their hands and knees paint with rice powder. The book *Painted Prayers: Women's Art in Village India* eloquently speaks of the value of immediacy of process and its connection to focus and faith. Hindu women in rural India have been passing on the tradition of ritual ground paintings to their daughters for hundreds of years. The ground paintings are created by women of all castes and have been adopted by Christians and Muslims as well. Women paint elaborate free-hand circular designs on the ground before their homes or a shrine; sometimes for special occasions, sometimes as an act of daily devotion. As they work, the women are focusing on family, community and faith. The whiteness of the rice powder is a symbol of purity and the sacred. Throughout the day it nourishes birds and insects and reminds family, friends and community of their shared values and beliefs.

Some guys in a local market decided the women were wasting too much of their time making ritual ground paintings. They invented a way to make a design quickly and efficiently. The men punched holes into PVC tubing in a geometric pattern. You just put the desired amount of rice powder in the tubing, place it on the ground and roll it (Huyler 1994, 18). Is this the same?

Is the process of making art as important to you as the product? Why? What is your focus when you make art? Do you focus on what is important to you?

The immediacy of the process of making art is an important reason many of us are artists. There is something fundamentally grounding and nurturing about working with your hands, which usually means your whole body. Feeling the clay, finding the proper physical balance and pressure to throw a pot, the diverse textures, colors, and light-reflective qualities of fiber, the rhythm of weaving, the gestures of drawing and painting that end in the hand but are felt throughout the body - these are experiences that help us to feel whole, vital, connected. In contrast, I find working at the computer sterile and cerebral. The body and senses are basically ignored, or are assaulted by mechanical voices and glaring colors.

The computers plastic keys are far removed from the earth, the natural, the fundamental. There is no denying that new technologies are exciting and hold many possibilities for us, but nonetheless after an initial exodus of students from art to computers, many art teachers are discovering that their classes are now filling with students who are heavily involved in the new technology, yet are realizing the importance of the basic connectedness of a physical creative process.

The physicality of making art reminds me of the physicality of Catholic worship. The sign of the cross, kneeling, genuflecting, holy water, chrism - how wonderful it is to know something with your whole being; body and soul. Many artists live this kind of knowing.

Weavers from many Moroccan Berber tribes create extremely intricate designs without seeing them, using the saha technique. The designs are on the front of the weaving, yet are woven from the reverse side, and are completely obscured by floats and ends during the weaving process. The designs are known so well by the weavers that they are completely integrated into their beings and done rapidly by feel, so that most of the time the process requires focus but not thought. A weaver named Aisha Sibwi once explained that she is aware of the threads "like a man who never counts his sheep but would know immediately if one were missing." She also said that once her fingers "lost the patterns." She went to her familial home and slept at the tomb of the local Muslim saint. The patterns were restored (Forelli, Harries 1977, 54). For Aisha Sibwi, and millions of others in diverse cultures around the world, process and faith are one.

The contemporary ceramic artist Brother Thomas Bezanson expresses this connection as an act of becoming in the video about his life and work, "Gifts from the Fire." He states, "Sometimes I say I am not really doing art, I am doing theology. It is a statement of hope. I am communicating those things that speak of God." He does not feel that his art work is complete until it is shared with others. He also says that creating his art "is not just about setting goals, external goals, but in trying to measure up to the internal goals, which constitute the real process of art." Brother Thomas had a dream earlier in his career of a white pot that was so simple and pure that it was almost not there and he pursued it for some time. Through the experiences he had when he visited Japan he came to understand "that the white pot was myself. I realized it was myself that I was trying to make pure, better, a more beautiful person, a more truthful person, a person concerned with uniting and not dividing what he encounters and meets along the journey in this world" (DEEGEE Productions 1991).

A student said that thinking about art in this way helped him to get back to his core. He was working as a machinist in a thankless job, had lived through tough times, recovered from alcoholism, and was helping others who were struggling. The intensity of his artwork for the class was breath-taking. The abstract imagery he used was transcendent, full of strength - tied to the spiritual core of his Dine heritage. At the semester's end, he told me he had quit his job and found another that allowed him to live his values more closely and that he was building a studio in his backyard, so that he could continue to bring what was important to him more fully into his life - through art.

There is a picture in *Painted Prayers* that moves me deeply. It shows a gray haired woman, bare feet on the ground, bending over in her sari, concentrating on the large, intricate, flowing pattern she is making with rice powder. The pattern is circular, about ten feet in diameter. Its center is a star that evolves into a looping design like the petals of a chrysanthemum, which flow into the shape of the tip of peacock feathers and then an outline reminiscent of lotus flowers. It is all done free-form through unified focus, is amazingly symmetrical, and takes about one hour. Like many women in her region, she does this every day. As people walk through it they are reminded of their family, community, and shared faith. Their feet carry with them her creation and disseminate the rice dust, the physical reminder of shared life, throughout the community. She has become for me a symbol of faith: deep and mature, committed, unwavering no matter what the day brings, constant in spite of the indifference or appreciation of others, shared with community, expressed physically and visually through a disciplined act of devotion; integrated into her very being.

The act of creation is also an act of becoming. Who we become through the process of creating is our choice.

Kizaemon Tea Bowl early 17th century, collection of Daitokuji.

Categories and Beauty: Art vs. Craft

Soetsu Yanagi (1889-1961) was a scholar, a curator, an advocate for Japanese folk art, a co-founder of the Mingei Association and the founder of the Japanese Folkcraft Museum in Tokyo. He did much to raise awareness of the value of folk art and inspired numerous artists; many of whom were designated National Living Treasures of Japan.

In *The Unknown Craftsman; A Japanese Insight into Beauty*, Yanagi makes many provocative statements on the nature of art and craft. Here are just a few:

> Surprisingly enough, the history of art is full of examples of the products of humble craftsmen that are finer than the work of clever individuals. This is because their work contains no signs of egotism. It is like looking for true belief in a world infested with self-centeredness. Only when egotism diminishes does true belief make an appearance (Yanagi 1972, 199).

> Objects that reveal ambition, objects in which lack of taste is knowingly simulated, objects where some quality such as strength or cleverness is exaggerated - these will not be universally admired for long, although they may create a momentary furor (Yanagi 1972, 143).

> All art movements tend to the pursuit of novelty, but the true essence of beauty can exist only where the distinction between the old and the new has been eliminated (Yanagi 1972, 131).

> Beauty is essentially a matter of values (Yanagi 1972, 111).

> To 'see' is to go direct to the core; to know the facts about an object of beauty is to go around the periphery (Yanagi 1972, 110).

> The principle of the beauty of craft is no different from the law that rules the spirit underlying all things. There is then no truer source than the words of religious scriptures. A true example of craft is the same as a passage of a holy scripture. Only in place of words, truth is conveyed through material, shape, colour, and pattern (Yanagi 1972, 215).

Do you believe there is a significant difference between art and craft? Why? Have you had the experience of "seeing" a work of art? What was the work and what did you "see"? What is beauty to you?

The art vs. craft debate, that attempts to define an art hierarchy through medium and technique, seems to me essentially artificial, but is taken seriously by many in the world of museums and galleries. We categorize in order to help articulate, yet too often lose sight of the essence of art and get lost in the empty structure we have created instead. Art is a bit like Suzuki's definition of Zen: "It is no abstraction; it is concrete enough, and direct, as the eye sees the sun is, but it is not subsumed in the categories of linguistics. As soon as we try to do this, it disappears" (Suzuki 1934, 7). For most of my students "art versus craft" is simply not an issue. Art exists to improve their lives and the material it is made of, the technique used, whether it is "functional" or "non-functional" is of relatively little importance. As more than one Native American student has told me, "There isn't a word in our culture for art, it is a part of life." The Tohono O'odham Basketweaver's Organization states this in its brochure. "Tohono O'odham weavers seek artful ways of living. In basketry, beauty and utility are joined together. Baskets unite the material, spiritual and aesthetic worlds. Some call it art. Most weavers simply call it life." Taking the art vs. craft debate seriously has to be "carefully taught."

Once when I was working on a series of pieces that were large, square, abstract weavings, a much respected friend and fellow Fiber artist brought forward this issue. The core of the weavings contained images and content similar to what an abstract painter might attempt with paint rather than thread. A strong unbroken band of color, I think of as the still point as defined in the traditions of prayer and meditation, is surrounded by broken color and abstracted imagery inspired by koi ponds, but is also intended to suggest the infinite; the beauty and wonder of creation. This core was surrounded by three sets of woven strips, carefully pieced and stitched together, that interacted with the core in color and pattern. My friend felt the work was "strong," but cautioned that the pieced borders were reminiscent of quilting and I may want to distance myself from that. Fiber art is intimately connected to women's art and the craft tradition. Very understandably distancing ourselves from these in order to participate in the world of contemporary art is considered by many to be our "reality." However, rather than succumbing to the status quo, it is my hope to bring what is valuable in the "craft" heritage to the "art" world;

changing our "reality."

This change in the way we view art, that I have long desired, was given a bit of reality in the exhibition *Made in California: Art, Image and Identity 1900-2000* at the Los Angeles County Museum of Art. It was an unprecedented museum-wide exhibit occupying 45,000 square feet of gallery space. I was thrilled to have a sculpture I had created in 1977 included in the exhibit. This work was part of a series I began in 1976 when I decided to explore sculptural form, other than the traditional container forms, through the basketry technique known as coiling. I created a series of spirals I called "Cycles," intended to give a sense of the infinite; an awareness of patience and perseverance. I was blessed to grow up in California during a time that fostered an openness to many cultures. Besides participating in the first African History class offered in a high school, I was also a student in one of the first Native American and African Art classes offered at the college level. I have long had an interest in Japan and like many California artists look across the ocean to the western horizon and the Pacific Rim for inspiration. I feel these influences are as apparent in my work as the European art tradition. My art work, like California, is a meeting place of many cultures, but bound by none. *Made in California* broke down the barriers of art vs. craft, and art greatly influenced by the European art tradition vs. art influenced by all the rest of the world. It was wonderful to see Native American baskets done early in the last century next to the landscape paintings of the same period. It was exhilarating to see David Hockney, Diego Rivera, Dorothea Lange, the designers Charles and Ray Eames, ceramic artist Laura Andreson, artists who took inspiration from the European psycho-analytic intellectual tradition and those who turn to Zen and elsewhere all sharing space; all giving voice to a diversified experience unified by California. The richer the diversity, the richer the dialogue. In this exhibit the dialogue was more important than the categories we create to define; the content of the work in the context of the last one hundred years of life in California was more important than art vs. craft. *Made in California* was the most major exhibition I have attended that represented a leap into art without boundaries, a sense of the intimate connection of art with life, that is similar to the direction the artists in this book have led me.

Since considering the lives and work of the artists in these chapters, the art vs. craft debate has lost all significance to me. For me, the success of an object lies solely in the value of the ideas it represents and its ability to communicate these ideas in the circumstances it is intended for. I once saw a tea bowl that spoke volumes to me. Yanagi writes: "Tea-bowls are not the project of the intellect. Yet their beauty is well defined, which is why it has been referred to both as the beauty of the imperfect and the beauty that deliberately rejects the perfect. Either way, it is a beauty lurking within. It is this beauty with inner implications that is referred to as shibui. It is not beauty displayed before the viewer by its creator; creation here means, rather, making a piece that will lead the viewer to draw beauty out of it for himself" (Yanagi 1972, 123-24). The tea bowl I saw gave me this experience. It was very simply made. It was modest in size and shape and the glaze was unobtrusive. The bowl was chipped a little on its rim, but it emanated a sense of great strength, humility, and peace; at once both transcendent and grounding. It had as much to communicate to me as any painting or sculpture. Perhaps this is what Yanagi calls "to see."

The Rothko Chapel in Houston, Texas, continues to be my most profound encounter of contemporary art. The chapel building is a simple brick octagon. It houses eight units, thirteen panels, of large abstract paintings by Mark Rothko, lit whenever possible by diffuse natural light. Rothko wrote in a letter to Dominique and John de Menil, who were the patrons of the chapel: "The magnitude, on every level of experience and meaning, of the task in which you have involved me, exceeds all my preconceptions. And it is teaching me to extend myself beyond what I thought was possible for me. For this I thank you" (Barnes 1996, 18). The paintings are very dark but they contain deep glowing complex colors. Rothko, who was of Russian Jewish heritage, once told Dominique de Menil that he wanted to create the same tension between doom and promise that he had experienced at the Byzantine basilica church of Saint Maria Assunta at Torcello, where he saw a mosaic of the Last Judgement and then the Madonna and Child on a golden background. I was gratified to read about this after I visited the chapel for the first time, for that is what I experienced.

I have never had such an overwhelming and powerful experience of the presence of God through a work of art as I had at the Rothko Chapel. The chapel spoke to me of the magnitude of our human failings and the suffering we have brought upon each other, holocaust upon holocaust. I felt this intensely and knew that in spite of my best intentions I was a part of this failing. Yet an awareness of God's profound, infinite, omnipotent grace left me awestruck. The comments in the visitors' book tell me I am not alone. It is usually a place of silence where people of many faiths go to pray and meditate. The Holy Books of diverse faiths are in the lobby for visitors to read from if they wish. It is also a place where different groups hold services, couples are married, colloquia are held, bringing together spiritual and intellectual leaders from around the world to explore such themes as "traditional modes of contemplation and action in world religions; human rights; new strategies for development in the Third World" (Barnes 1996, 15). Nelson Mandela and many others have received The Carter-Menil Human Rights Award here. The Rothko Chapel is truly ecumenical. Rothko once said, "The people who weep before my pictures are having the same religious experience I had when I painted them, and if you, as you say, are moved only by their color relationships you miss the point!" (Barnes 1996, 22). Although very abstract, through the force of the chapel's intent, the vision of its patrons and the strength of the artist's focus, the Rothko Chapel is accessible to people of many faiths and enriches their perceptions of art, life, and faith.

I find the Rothko Chapel profoundly beautiful. I believe in beauty. As with both the tea bowl and the Rothko Chapel beauty needn't be easy. Yanagi wrote, "The principle of the beauty of craft is no different from the law that rules the spirit underlying all things...A true example of craft is the same as a passage of holy scripture" (Yanagi 1972, 215). Suzuki says this in a somewhat different way: "Some critics state that all great works of art embody in them yugen whereby we attain a glimpse of things eternal in the world of constant changes..." (Suzuki 1970, 220). A document on Environment and Art in Catholic Worship states: "Admittedly difficult to define, the beautiful is related to the sense of the numinous, the holy" (Bishops' Committee 1977, 325). To see in this way is a pursuit I do not tire of; it brings a gratitude for life that cannot be contained. I give thanks for my eyes everyday. Gaining an understanding of beauty, like conversion, is never ending; an endeavor for a lifetime.

The tea bowl and the Rothko Chapel were created in a spirit of humility. Both artists were reaching for timeless universal values beyond self-expression. The fact that one is old, the other new, one is "functional," the other "fine art," is insignificant. Their beauty comes from the values they represent, brought to life through the focus and intent of the artist and the awareness of the viewer. Or, as it sometimes seems, our experience of a work of art has less to do with our own awareness and is instead, wholly or partially, a revelation; a gift of grace. Old or new, clay or canvas, woven or painted, "craft" or "fine art," all art is functional when it brings life; dysfunctional when it does not.

Juanita Serrano with Santo Nino de Atocha by Louis Carlos Bernal.

Conclusion

So what does it mean to create with reverence? To create with reverence is to give life to values that magnify the soul. Artists create with reverence when they choose such values to be the focus of their lives and work. Their focus becomes physically manifest in their creations and, through the process of creating, is amplified in their beings. Their lives and work become prayer. This is a timeless view of art, shared by people of many cultures and faiths, that is a gift to us all.

The artists in this book represent many cultures, yet all live this way of creating. Their stories challenge and expand our perspective of art.

Significant art needn't be only for galleries and museums. The Mayan weavers of Chiapas, Mexico, show us what it might mean for the act of creating to be so thoroughly integrated with life, with heritage, community and faith, that there is no division. They reveal to us the strength and rewards of committing to wearing our heart on our sleeve.

The relevance of art is much more than self-expression. Maria Martinez was a highly gifted individual who never separated herself from community and who used her gift to bring to life community values and to serve her community.

The image of the artist as an isolated individual somehow above and separate from community is limiting and deceiving. Chuck Kaparich had a deep appreciation of the inextricable collaboration and continuity of generations. He helped a community to live this awareness by creating a living symbol of gratitude.

Creating for friends and family has significant consequences, the ripple effect in action, and can serve humanity as much as "serious art." The pioneering quilters of Arizona knew the importance of prolonged focus on life giving values; the connection between something lovingly made by hand and breath for the soul.

Freedom of expression is often confused with "anything goes." True freedom comes through limiting our choices and using resources wisely, in a way that helps us to live values that matter. The women of many Native American nations created this way.

A disregard of craftsmanship should not be taken lightly. Good craftsmanship is the manifestation of important ideas and values. The woodworkers of Kyoto, Japan, embody the principles of Tea in every aspect of their craftsmanship and the objects of integrity they make.

Creating quickly is not necessarily a virtue. Time to reflect gives direction to our experiences, deepens insight and helps us to live. Both Shaker and Japanese craftsmen understood the timeless gift of an act of total attention, where there is no division between head, heart, and hands.

To live reverently we must use cultural information wisely and respectfully. The paintings of the Aborigines of Utopia eloquently demonstrate the power of art that is from the soul of the artist and honest to her experience. They represent cultural appropriation at its best; celebrating diversity and challenging us to hold on to what is important together.

Art of despair essentially joins what it purports to abhor. Hiroshima Kazuo's decision to overcome adversity through humbly serving his community is an inspiration to choose our focus well and reconsider what "strength" is.

Art can be more than commentary on contemporary culture. The devotional ground paintings made by women in village India illuminate our understanding of how an act of creation can also be an act of becoming and an act of faith.

Creating categories of art can help us to articulate, but can also lead us to lose sight of what is important. We need to commit to the value of what we express, not to perceived categories. The insights of Soetsu Yanagi, honed through his lifelong interest in Japanese folk art, challenge our ideas about art and beauty, opening the way to a more profound understanding of art that brings life.

The act of creating has many potential rewards. Through prolonged focus on values that matter we give life to those values. This is evident in the stories of my students: the young woman who wove a series of purses that personified her most important friendships; the elderly woman, confined by heart problems, who paints pictures of family heritage; the students from Appalachia who cherish the memory of the quilts their mothers made from feed-bag strips; the many students who bring an understanding they have gained through creating to others - at-risk youth, children, seniors, faith communities - by applying their talents to community projects. Experiencing and understanding an act of total attention helped a recent divorcee find answers she didn't even know she was seeking and sustained a young woman who was homeless. Students of many backgrounds have realized the relevance of holding onto what is important together through their art and through tangible symbols, such as the bowl and card given to me. The opportunity to reflect, to manifest, to become, and to give the gift of life, is arts' promise when we create with reverence.

Reflecting on what this means has enriched my own life in many ways. Making the decision to more openly wear my heart on my sleeve has imbued my work experience with a greater awareness of the sacred that was not there before. I am more conscious of community and my desire to share community values, both through my art work and in collaborative projects such as the Easter banner. I am more cognizant of the potential of creative acts and physical symbols in my everyday family life. Through an expanded awareness of the significance of craftsmanship, an act of total attention, and the Shakers' ideas on time, I know deeper fulfillment when creating. Acts of faith now permeate my creative process. My art is more focused, there are fewer failures. Where I was once a bit burnt out when teaching, art is now alive. My students are more responsive and share in ways I didn't know were possible on a daily basis. Being with them is a joy. Art, life and faith are more consciously a whole.

As is so often the case, my understanding of the significance of our decisions was heightened through coming to terms with a tragedy. My friend, the photographer Lou Bernal, was struck by a car, driven by one of our mutual students, when he was riding his bike to teach at the college where we both worked. For four years I visited him while he was in a coma, until he died on his fifty-second birthday in 1993. In the years since, the legacy of his work, his life choices, has been striking. I have met seemingly countless students, professionals, people from all walks of life whom he continues to inspire. Ten years after his death, the gallery at our college was officially named after him and hundreds of people attended the dedication.

Those of us who create have a choice. What we surround ourselves with and how and what we create make a palpable difference. The physical is a manifestation of ideas and values in a very real sense, that affects all our lives. Our choices matter.

Do we support icons of consumerism in what we wear or do we commit to symbols of life-giving values? Do we choose self-expression alone or do we serve community? Do we perpetuate the myth of the totally self-realized individual or do we acknowledge our debt to others, express our gratitude and provide for future generations? Do we choose to be the isolated iconoclast or to connect with those around us? Do we spend our resources on being the ultimate consumers or surround ourselves with objects of integrity? Do we get lost in "freedom of choice" or do we hone our focus through limitation? Do we use resources arrogantly or respectfully? Does our art work invite knee-jerk reaction or reflection and conversion? Do we slow down enough to allow ourselves to experience an act of total attention? Do we take our knowledge of other cultures and render what has meaning to others into something essentially meaningless, or do we learn from each other and hold on to what is important together? When facing difficult issues in our art, do we perpetuate despair or enlighten? Do we choose to fit into art history or develop and exercise integrity? Is our act of creation an act of devotion and faith? Do we limit ourselves through categories or seek beauty without limitations? Do we choose art that is merely contemporary or art that is timeless? Do we live and create with reverence?

In *Zen and Japanese Culture*, D.T. Suzuki relates this legend about the swordsmith Masamune Okazaki:

> Masamune flourished in the latter part of the Kamakura era, and his works are uniformly prized by all the sword connoisseurs for their excellent qualities. As far as the edge of the blade is concerned, Masamune may not exceed Muramasa, one of his ablest disciples, but Masamune is said to have something morally inspiring that comes from his personality. The legend goes thus: When someone was trying to test the sharpness of a Muramasa, he placed it in a current of water and watched how it acted against the dead leaves flowing downstream. He saw that every leaf that met the blade was cut in twain. He then placed a Masamune, and he was surprised to find that the leaves avoided the blade. The Masamune was not bent on killing, it was more than a cutting implement, whereas the Muramasa could not go beyond cutting, there was nothing divinely inspiring it. The Muramase is terrible, the Masamune is humane (Suzuki 1970:92).

May we choose to create instruments of peace, become instruments of peace, create with reverence and give life to all that is sacred.

Lord make me an instrument of Thy peace.
Where there is hatred, let me sow love.
where there is injury, pardon;
where there is doubt, faith;
where there is despair, hope;
where there is darkness, light;
where there is sadness, joy.

Grant that I may not so much seek to be consoled as to console,
to be understood as to understand,
to be loved as to love.

For it is in giving that we receive,
it is in pardoning that we are pardoned,
and it is in dying that we are born to eternal life.

Prayer of Saint Francis

Hózhóogo naasháa doo
Shitsijí' hózhóogo naasháa doo
Shikéédéé hózhóogo naasháa doo
Shideigi hózhóogo naasháa doo
T'áá altso shinaagóó hózhóogo naasháa doo
Hózhó náhásdlíí'
Hózhó náhásdlíí'
Hózhó náhásdlíí'
Hózhó náhásdlíí'

In beauty I walk
With beauty before me I walk
With beauty behind me I walk
With beauty above me I walk
With beauty around me I walk
It has become beauty again
It has become beauty again
It has become beauty again
It has become beauty again

Closing Prayer from the Dine (Navajo) Blessing Way Ceremony

Bibliography

Australian Government, Director of National Parks. *Uluru-Kata Tjuta National Park; Visitor Guide*. 2006.

Barnes, Susan J. *The Rothko Chapel: An Act of Faith*. Houston, Texas: The Rothko Chapel, 1996.

Barron, Stephanie; Sheri Bernstein and Ilene Susan Fort. *Made in California: Art, Image and Identity 1900-2000*. Berkeley: Los Angeles County Museum of Art and University of California Press, 2000.

Bishops' Committee on the Liturgy. *Environment and Art In Catholic Worship*. Washington, DC: United States Catholic Conference of Publishing and Promotion Services, 1977. Publication No. 563-1.

Boulter, Michael. *The Art of Utopia: A New Direction in Contemporary Aboriginal Art*. Roseville East, Australia: Craftsman House, 1993.

Brafford, C.J. and Laine Thom. *Dancing Colors: Paths of Native American Women*. San Francisco: Chronicle Books, 1992.

Cort, Louise Allison and Kenji Nakamura. *A Basketmaker in Rural Japan*. Washington, D.C.: Arthur M. Sackler Gallery, 1994.

Cross, S., director. *The Traditional World of Islam: Nomad and City*. (film) AMOCO, 1976.

DEEGEE Productions, Del Prete, Deborah and Gigi Pritzker. *Gifts From The Fire: The Ceramic Art Of Brother Thomas*. (video) 1991.

Devlin, Sherry; Thomas Bauer and John Engen. *A Carousel for Missoula*. Missoula, Montana: The Missoulian, 1995.

Diamond, Inc. *The Traditional Crafts of Japan "Kyoto Joinery"*. Tokyo, Japan, (video) 1992.

Forelli, Sally and Jeanette Harries. "Traditional Berber Weaving in Central Morocco." *The Textile Museum Journal* vol.IV, no.4 (1977): 41-60.

Frost, Helen Young and Pam Knight Stevenson. *Grand Endeavors: Vintage Quilts and Their Makers*. Flagstaff, Arizona: Northland Publishing, 1992.

Huyler, Stephen P. *Painted Prayers: Women's Art in Village India*. New York: Rizzoli, 1994.

Mingei International Museum. *Kindred Spirits: The Eloquence of Function in American Shaker and Japanese Arts of Daily Life*. San Diego: Mingei International, 1995.

Morris, Walter F. Jr., text and Jeffrey J. Foxx, photographs. *Living Maya*. New York: Harry N. Abrams, Inc., 1987.

Neill, Hope. *HOPE A Continual Dreaming*. (exhibition brochure) Brisbane: Metro Arts, 1993.

Ross, Doran H. *Wrapped in Pride: Ghanaian Kente and African American Identity.* Los Angeles: UCLA Fowler Museum of Cultural History and the Newark Museum, 1998.

Simmons-Myers, Ann. *Louis Carlos Bernal: Barrios.* Tucson: University of Arizona Press, 2002.

Soshitsu Sen XV. *Tea Life, Tea Mind.* New York: Weatherhill, 1979.

Spivey, Richard L. *Maria.* Flagstaff, Arizona: Northland Publishing, 1979.

Suzuki, Daisetz Teitaro. *The Training of the Zen Buddhist Monk.* New York: Globe Press Books, 1934.

Suzuki, Daisetz Teitaro. *Zen and Japanese Culture.* Princeton University Press, 1970.

Uchida, Yoshiko. *We Do Not Work Alone: the Thoughts of Kanjiro Kawai.* Kyoto: Nissha Printing Company, Ltd., 1973.

Urasenke Foundation. *The Urasenke Tradition of Tea.* Kyoto: Urasenke Foundation, 1993.

Wright, Tom, text and Mizuno Katsuhiko, photographs. *Zen Gardens: Kyoto's Nature Enclosed.* Kyoto: Mitsumura Suiko Shoin Co., Ltd., 1994.

Yanagi, Soetsu. *The Unknown Craftsman: A Japanese Insight Into Beauty.* Tokyo, New York, London: Kodansha International, 1972.

Acknowledgments

This book would not be possible without the encouragement and suggestions of my readers; Diane Bridenbecker OP, Renilde Cade OP, Elissa Cahn, Mark Cesnik, Louise Allison Cort, Doris Klein CSA, Tom Lundberg, Norma Mendoza-Denton, Ursula Nakai, Josephine Ramirez, Jane Sauer, Michael Schiffer, Alice Schlegel, and Stephanie Sikora. I am also thankful for the inspiration of Judith Ransom Miller and Kathleen Rose OP, the editing of Diane Luber, and the support of friends and colleagues Meg Files, Sharon Takeda, Hirotsune Tashima and Erin Younger.

Many photographers gave generously of their time and inspiring images; my thanks especially to Jeffrey Jay Foxx, Stephen Huyler, Robinder Uppal, Lisa Bernal Brethour and Katrina Bernal. I sincerely appreciate those who helped research image copyrights; Kristi Ehrig-Burgess, Laraine Jones, and Alice Hart.

My unending thanks to my husband Tad who has spent hundreds of hours as my foremost consultant and as an indispensable technology guru.

Made in the USA
Lexington, KY
07 December 2010